Islam in Europe

To Robert Hinde,
Partha Dasgupta,
compagnons de route,
and to all those other Fellows
of St John's who have
helped with my enquiries

ISLAM IN EUROPE

Jack Goody

polity

The right of Jack Goody to be identified as Author of this
Work has been asserted in accordance with the UK Copyright,
Designs and Patents Act 1988.

First published in 2004 by Polity Press in association with
Blackwell Publishing Ltd.

Reprinted 2005

Polity Press
65 Bridge Street
Cambridge CB2 1UR, UK

Polity Press
350 Main Street
Malden, MA 02148, USA

A catalogue record for this book is available from the British Library.

Library of Congress Cataloging-in-Publication Data

Goody, Jack.
Islam in Europe / Jack Goody.
      p. cm.
   Includes bibliographical references and index.
   ISBN 0-7456-3192-4 – ISBN 0-7456-3193-2 (pbk.)
   1. Islam – Europe.   2. Muslims – Europe.   3. East and West.
   4. Terrorism – Religious aspects – Islam.   I. Title.
   BP65.A1G66 2004
   297′.094–dc21   2003009840

Typeset in 11 on 13 pt Berling
by Graphicraft Limited, Hong Kong
Printed and bound in Great Britain
by TJ International, Padstow, Cornwall

For further information on Polity, visit our website: www.polity.co.uk

Contents

List of Maps

Preface

This short book has a number of origins. The Near East has long had an interest for me, ever since I found myself as a young man in the midst of Arab–Israeli and Greek–Turkish conflicts in the 1940s, conflicts that were partly suppressed at that time in the context of the wider struggle with the Axis powers. Returning to Cyprus many years later, in the company of Paul Sant Cassia, I was, like all other visitors, struck by the greater divide that now existed between the Muslim Turks and the Christian Greeks, in which it seemed that religion played a much stronger part than most social scientists allowed. That also seemed to be the case in the Balkans and was obviously so in Israel/Palestine. As a result of writing about this situation, I was asked to give a talk on Islam in Europe to a Socialist History Group in London, no doubt because their own approach saw religious differences as much less important than class ones, just as others saw them as 'expressions' of 'ethnicity' or 'identity'. That effort at explanation led to my trying to clarify, in a simple and all too brief essay, the contacts and influences that Islam had had with Europe. Finding that religion generally and Islam in particular had been down-played, I wanted to show something of the nature of the interactions between Islam and Europe, taking seriously the actors' view of the situation.

Preface

That desire was reinforced in the aftermath of 11 September 2001, when Islam was increasingly seen as the enemy Other. I aimed to show that it was also part and parcel of the European past and present. And to do so from a generalist's standpoint, for a non-specialist audience.

A version of the second chapter appeared in the *New Left Review*, vol. 7 (2001), and as revised in *History and Anthropology*, vol. 13 (2002), 1–12. A version of chapter 3 appeared in the latter journal, vol. 13 (2002), 139–43. I would like to thank John Kerrigan, Richard Beadle, Jocelyne Dakhlia, Murray Last, Richard Hodges, Nicole Rousmanière, Javier Ribas, Ulinka Rublack, Gilbert Lewis, Roxanna Waterson, Dionigi Albera, Peter Linehan, Caroline Humphrey and Ziba Mir-Hosseini, who provided references or who read chapters. I am grateful to Nile Green, Jessica Bloom, Melanie Hales and Susan Mansfield for their help in preparing the text.

Introduction

'A spectre is haunting Europe.' This is not the spectre of communism to which Marx and Engels were referring but rather the spectre of Islam and Islamic 'terrorism'. With Marx and Engels we can say that 'All the Powers of Old Europe have entered into a holy alliance to exorcise this spectre: Pope and Czar, Metternich and Guizot, French Radicals and German police spies.' We can easily translate the latter into their modern equivalents and add the USA, Russia, China, India and elsewhere. But is the comprehension of the spectre any greater? I wrote what I present here as a contribution to an understanding of the place of Islam in Europe's past and present around the time of the attack on the Twin Towers in New York. Islam and Muslims had generally had a bad press in the West well before that time, but that tragedy has dramatically worsened the situation. The American president, George Bush, is notorious for having used the word 'crusade' in relation to the 'war against terrorism', thus defining it as a war of the Cross against the Crescent, of Christianity, or in his case of Judaeo-Christian civilization, against Islam. As such it becomes a 'holy war' (*jihad*), at least metaphorically, reverting to medieval and early modern perceptions.[1] Terrorism, Islamic terrorism, is something to be eradicated at all costs, even at the expense

1

of a war pursued if 'necessary' outside the rules of war and of the United Nations (by 'pre-emptive strikes'), since the existence of 'terrorism' is a threat to America. In the USA early in 2002 one was constantly being handed flags to display, often on one's car, or else badges of the Stars and Stripes to wear in one's lapel. On the rear window of many private cars appeared banners with the words 'God Bless America'. As in the early days of the colony, God was seen to be firmly on the side of the Americans, helping them to defeat the Indians so the latter would become civilized and Christian. The notion of Christianizing the heathen has been given up as a political strategy, no doubt in view of the fact that Islam shows no sign of retreating – quite the contrary. Nevertheless Bush is constantly calling upon God to back the United States in pursuit of her foreign policy. Religion is constantly brought into the picture.

There is an idea abroad that, of the world's major religions, only Islam persists in the idea of a holy war. It is true that, with the increasing secularization that followed the Renaissance, much of Europe has been more tolerant about religion. Nevertheless the wars and struggles between Catholics and Protestants were frighteningly savage. Following the Enlightenment the situation changed. But much of the ideology behind the extensive colonial expansion of that continent was Christian in tone and was accompanied by hordes of missionaries penetrating into every corner of the world. With the backing of the colonial powers and their armies, they had no need to use force themselves. The conquest had already been done for them. In Islam, on the other hand, leadership of the state and the religion are ideally combined in one person, so all wars are religious wars.

The USA suffered a severe blow on 11 September 2001, a blow that literally came out of the blue, unexpected, unpredicted, unprecedented, in a country that sees itself as far removed from the front line. But the use of the term 'terrorist' seemed to suggest an enemy whose only purpose was the use of violence for undiscernible ends. That usage distracted attention from the question of whether there was any political, social or religious aim behind the acts, and whether the perpetrators saw themselves as having alternative means of pursuing them. It distracted attention from the way that a good part of the rest of the world contemplates the situation of a single superpower which possesses an immense preponderance of military and economic might, so that one way or another it can command, assert or impose its will on other parts of the world. Such preponderance of unequal resources inevitably encourages resistance and opposition. The positioning of troops in the Near East, especially in Arabia, the support given to its satellite Israel, the scramble for oil, these are particular foci of resentment. And while in most cases that resentment does not issue in active forms, it can always do so, leading to a violence which employs similar notions of 'holy war' to that implicit, and often explicit, in the actions of the West, though there the sacred aims are phrased in terms of liberty, democracy, the free market, rarely in terms of equality or fraternity. If this analysis is remotely correct, it means that, while 'the war on terrorism' may undoubtedly gain its local victories, the resistance itself will emerge again and again. A defeat in Afghanistan is followed by a devastating blast in Bali, a mass kidnapping in Moscow, perhaps even a sniper in Washington. Hydra-headed, it will emerge in one form or another while the problem exists, the problem that rarely receives an adequately comprehensive analysis and that demands a socio-political solution, rather than armed conflict or the raising of cries of terrorism among all the non-Islamic powers, Europe, Russia, India and China, as well as the United States. All states wish to control resentful minorities.

In America, it has been held that the attacks of 11 September had nothing to do with its policy towards Israel. That is plainly wrong, as Bin Laden has made clear. Other attacks against Western powers, not apparently associated with al-Qaeda, have given as justification the same reason. 'Terrorism' of this kind will persist as long as the situation does. Until the West adopts different attitudes towards the desires of many Muslims regarding penetration into the Near East,

3

attacks will continue. The war on terrorism will never end and occupation of countries in the area such as Iraq can only aggravate the tensions, not eliminate them. The comparison between post-war Germany and Japan is quite misleading; Islam is not a form of fascism, whatever its tactics. You have to come to terms with a movement of this kind, just as whites had to come to terms with blacks in South Africa and in the American South.

A commentator on the Iranian revolution recently wrote: 'All through the twentieth century the modern world has wanted to bury religion at the level of an individual's private life. Now, for some decades, one has seen a return in strength of ostentatious religions, which threaten the public space they occupy, break with society and are in a struggle against it' (Khosrokhavar 2002: 7). That revolution has had its impact far and wide, for it is seen as being of global signi-ficance not simply for Islam but in the effort to combat globalization especially in its American form, represented for them by the alliance of petrol companies, of rulers (like the Shah) and of American interests. Here 'petro-Islam' is the key; it is not accidental that the Islamic revolution should have taken place in petrol-rich Iran or that the leader of al-Qaeda should be a child of a petrol economy. The irony is that the Western world, with its vast consumption of energy, requires Middle Eastern oil, a demand that makes those countries (or their leaders) rich and creates conditions for political interference to maintain the supplies without which their dominating economies would collapse. In other words, economically as well as politically they provide the background for Islamic (and particularly Arab) resistance and 'terrorism'. One of the complaints against the regimes of these countries was that the rulers make little attempt to distribute their wealth to poorer members of the faith, in accord with the Qur'an. The great disparities of wealth, the attachment to consumerism, the American political and milit-ary domination in the Holy Lands, above all their support of an invading Israel in the Near East, these were and are greatly contentious issues, which have their repercussions in the cities of Europe. Iran and al-Qaeda are often seen as standing bravely against those influences (which they can do with their access to petrol-dollars). While the USA regards them as part of 'an axis of evil', they regard the USA as 'the evil empire'.

The swift characterization of Islamic groups as 'terrorist' led to a neglect of their political and social agenda, whether this was a struggle for independence in Palestine and Kashmir or the attempt to force Western powers out of the oil-rich Arabian peninsula sacred to Islam. These struggles were carried out under conditions of devastating military inferiority (for example, while Israel has nuclear weapons and the latest aircraft, the Islamic powers of the Near East do not).[2] This inferiority in weaponry is accompanied by a deep sense of injustice. In the course of the Arab revolt in the First World War, the Arabs, encouraged by among others T. E. Lawrence, looked forward to their own nationhood, whereas they had previously been submerged under the Turkish empire. The Arabs maintain that the independence of Palestine was included in the promises embodied in the exchange of correspondence in July to October 1915 between Sir Henry McMahon, High Commissioner of Egypt, and Husayn ibn Ali, the Emir of Mecca. In 1917, as a result of the declaration by Lord Balfour to Lord Rothschild, Palestine was declared to be 'a national home for Jewish people' with the proviso that nothing be done to prejudice the rights of the other inhabitants, of which in 1914 there were some 605,000 compared with 85,000 Jews. Article 22 of the Covenant of the League of Nations, signed in June 1919, recognized 'the provisional independence' of the former Ottoman provinces, subject to the assistance of the mandatory power. For the conquering Western powers, Britain and France, had arranged for Palestine, the Lebanon and Syria to become mandated territories allocated to them by the League of Nations so that they could monitor their interests in the Near East and above all over the Suez Canal. Britain then permitted a certain level of Jewish immigration, which later greatly increased during the Nazi pogroms of the 1930s and the genocide of the 1940s. However, the majority of the population never accepted this situation and the Syrian Congress of 1920 had decisively rejected the Balfour Declaration and elected Faysal king of a united Syria that included Palestine. That initiative was stopped when, at the San Remo conference in the same year, the victorious allies divided up those Ottoman territories as quasi-colonial mandates, forcing Faysal to give up Syria to the French. And in that very year Palestinian riots against the Jewish settlers were attributed to the disappointment of the Arabs over their failure to achieve independence.

The penetration of Israel into the Near East can be seen as a newer version of the Crusades, carried out on behalf of the European Jewish community. It could not have happened if the Christian powers, specifically Britain, had not taken over part of the region as 'mandated' territory after the First World War. The Balfour Declaration of 1917 enabled the Jews to fulfil the longstanding dream of exiles: 'Next year in Jerusalem', or at least in Tel Aviv.

Under the British mandate Jewish immigration and land purchases continued, heavily financed from abroad. So too did inter-communal conflicts. In 1935 the British authorities tried to introduce certain 'democratic' institutions, in which the Arabs would have fourteen seats, the Jews eight, but this proposal was rejected by the latter even though the proportions were highly favourable to them; for they feared that majority rule might inhibit migration and hence their future dominance. Only after that was achieved did they become 'democratic'. Another fully fledged Arab revolt began the following year which was attributed to their fear of the country becoming a Jewish national home. As a result of the Peel enquiry into the causes of this revolt, partition was proposed, a solution that was adopted in principle by the League of Nations, suggesting an independent Arab state within ten years. But the two parties themselves disagreed, each wanting all or nothing. By 1939 the Jews formed 30 per cent of the population, much to the Arabs' resentment. At the end of the Second World War the UK and the USA proposed provincial autonomy for the two sides, while the new United Nations actually favoured partition together with the internationalization of Jerusalem. The demand for Palestinian statehood is therefore nothing new; it had been talked about for some eighty years. The talks had always proved frustrating to the Palestinians, partly because the Israelis had strong outside support from the very beginning, and that included military provisions; they were better organized for violence, later by the new state of Israel, earlier of the 'terrorist' kind. They were also seen as interlopers in the Near East, as were the French and British mandates, together with the further European penetration in search of oil. The Israelis played football with Europe (not Asia), joined in the European song contest and were treated (and saw themselves) as a democratic European power as well as an American dependency. Meanwhile Islam was the other, the enemy, always the disturbing faction.

That view of Islam picks up on earlier attitudes. The Crusades had been seen by the West as completely legitimate, while *jihads* were a form of reprehensible violence directed against us as the infidel. Both were holy wars. Each party was inevitably the other's unbeliever, lacking the true faith, a situation that persists today in discussions of who is a terrorist. But is there anything more terrorizing than aerial bombardment which kills thousands of civilians, including women and children? In addition to its addiction to terrorism, Islam is viewed as being socio-culturally backward, though it has the same roots as Judaism and Christianity, from whose company it is often excluded by the widespread concept of the uniqueness of Judaeo-Christian civilization. Economically backward Islamic countries may be in contrast to Europe after the changes in modes of production embodied in the Industrial Revolution, or even after the changes in the modes of communication following the introduction to the West of the printing press. But, at an earlier stage, Europe had had a lot to learn from Islamic science, technology and even from aspects of its arts. Even Muslim iconoclasm, recently much condemned in the imagistic West, had its roots in the common scriptures of the Near Eastern religions (chapter 4).

The direction of this book is unlikely to find much favour in the ruling circles of the great powers, all of whom have struggled with Muslim groups over recent years, the USA because of the over-riding support it has given to the establishment of the (Jewish) state of Israel on what for 1500 years had been Muslim lands, Russia and China because of the influence that Islam had had over the centuries in southern Russia and in north-west China and that has produced many hidden tensions and open conflicts. My thesis here is, yes, Islam is a different religion, with its own preoccupations, but, while it is often excluded from the Judaeo-Christian tradition, it is in fact essentially intrinsic to it – hence the perpetual problem of Jerusalem claimed by all three creeds, now and in the past. But even without the recent immigrants to Europe from Pakistan (in the UK), from North Africa (in France) and from Turkey (in Germany) that supply such an important part of the labour force, the role of Islam has been of great importance not only to but in Europe itself ever since the eighth century, in terms of its political, military and religious presence as well as for what it has contributed to technology, architecture, classical scholarship, mathematics, chemistry, agriculture, the use of water, philosophy, political science, travel literature and indeed literature more generally.

In this context I wanted to remind the Europeans that, whatever the problems with Islam, they were not only to be seen as attached to the 'backward' other. Islam has played a significant role in Europe since its advent in Spain and the Mediterranean in the eighth century, followed by its advance into Eastern Europe in the fourteenth and its movement into the northern steppes soon afterwards. Today all Western nations include literally millions of Muslims. To damp down potential conflict we need to understand something of the past and present of this religion, as well as of its politico-religious agenda. We need to suspend our disbelief, whether in Islam or in religions generally, in order to be able to assess the aims and implications of this highly successful world-wide creed and to treat its practitioners as one of the Peoples of the Book as well as of Europe itself.

Jack Goody

St John's College, Cambridge, 2003

1

Past Encounters

My initial interest in the theme of Islam in Europe goes
back to a long-standing inquisitiveness about Islam in the
Mediterranean and North Africa and its influence on West
Africa, where I lived and worked for many years. More
specifically it has roots in a concern with a number of conflicts in Europe and the role of religious affiliation in some
serious disputes in the contemporary world, a role that I
thought had been played down by many recent discussants.
These analysts often came from intellectual circles that had
themselves rejected religion as a personal faith and assumed
that others had done (or should do) the same. I felt this
was true of some important intellectuals who had examined
nationalism, for instance, Ernest Gellner and Eric Hobsbawm,
who paid little or no attention to religion, which was often
treated under the vague blanket term ethnicity, or even
identity, terms which I argued had little empirical reference.
That neglect of religion was especially associated with un-
committed Jews as well as non-practising Christians, and of
course with those many socialists who approved the Soviet
constitution of 1917 which announced 'the abolition of all
national and national-religious prejudices and restrictions,
and the full development of national minorities and ethnic
groups'. Similar aims either of religious freedom or freedom

from religion were proclaimed by the English Revolution of 1649, by the American Revolution of 1787 and by the French Revolution (and its Napoleonic successor) of 1789. Nevertheless religion remained a significant factor not simply in assisting national struggles but in formulating them. Its power of resistance is outstanding, as with the Orthodox church in the USSR and its later revival, and as we see from Islamic resistance to that country in Afghanistan and in the current struggle in Chechnya, as well as in the historic divisions and the terrible 'ethnic cleansings' in Northern Ireland, in India and Pakistan and in Israel, in all of which cases we have evidence of the persistence of religious affiliation and perhaps to a lesser extent of religious belief in shaping these long-continuing conflict situations. We cannot understand contemporary Palestine nor for that matter what happened in New York on 9/11 simply under the rubric of 'terrorism' or 'ethnicity' without taking into account the profound religious dimension. Islam impinges directly on all our lives, now as in the past, ever since its establishment in Arabia at the beginning of the seventh century.

I want to say something of that past, but first the present, a topic to which I will return in greater detail. There are today some two million Muslims in Germany (mainly from Turkey), the same number in Britain (mostly from the Indian sub-continent), some six million in France (mostly from North Africa), and some fifteen million in the European Union, even before its projected expansion eastwards; the numbers are in all cases uncertain. These substantial minorities have important social and political implications for the respective societies, especially as the communities are made up of recent immigrants who differ not only in their religion but in other cultural ways, who maintain their distance and distinctiveness (as well as having them maintained) and hence provide fuel for xenophobic and what is often called racist reaction but which has a very strong element of religious prejudice. They provide cultural diversity but also constitute points of divergence from common norms. Bans on immigrants will not affect these numbers. Their size might suggest a substantial influence on the political process, but they are of course dispersed (and many dispossessed) and our type of democracy does not really allow independent representation. Unlike the wealthy Jewish lobby in the USA, these Muslims can do relatively little directly to affect national policies towards the Near East and elsewhere. Nevertheless they are beginning to make an impact. In England Muslims have demonstrated over Kashmir, an act that was interpreted as showing a concern with homeland issues rather than integrating into British politics (an accusation never made against Jewish groups demonstrating about Israel). In terms of direct influence on the political process, they are largely impotent. Partly as a result of this perceived impotence, they provided recruits for the Taliban and al-Qaeda and before that for the Afghan national struggle against occupation by the USSR, where 'terrorism' and 'extremism' emerged seamlessly from the national liberation struggle.

The history of Islam and Europe displays three broad currents of territorial penetration that have affected that continent since the very beginning of the Muslim religion in the seventh century. And Islam in turn was one of the three streams of Near Eastern religion that have affected Europe in the Common Era. In the Roman period there was the dispersion of the Jews (and Carthaginians) throughout the empire, to Italy, to Spain, to France and then more widely. There was Christianity from about the same period, but mainly after the conversion of Constantine in 313 CE, spreading out from its Roman stronghold. And there was the Islamic expansion beginning only three centuries later. The three currents of Islam to which I referred were the Maghribian (the Arab), the Balkan (the Ottoman Turkish) and the Northern European (the Mongol), and their rough dates are the eighth, the fourteenth and again the fourteenth century (as Muslims, after conversion). Each of the three Muslim thrusts made their mark on the thinking of Western Europe. There was the recognition of Islamic learning, its luxuries and its military achievements. The last posed a threat in the minds of people far away from the front line that is still embodied

12

in linguistic usage. Just as the campaigns of earlier conquerors from the East have left their mark on the European vocabulary of devastation, in particular through the Huns and the Vandals, so too the Mongol thrust left its mark on English with 'he's a real Tartar' for a destructive child; the Turkish advance gave us 'a little Turk' for the same infant, while the Moors gave rise to 'street Arab'. Moreover both the Turks and the Moors left their impact on village fêtes that embodied Turks and blackamoors in their performances.[1] According to Primo Levi, the word *Musulman* came to be used in Nazi concentration camps for inmates who 'gave up'. This long and massive penetration has been frequently neglected in the West. Historians have much to answer for as far as this aspect of Europe is concerned. To a large degree that continent is their creation as they have seen it as a boundary-maintaining region, a continent defined by an ancestry reaching back to Greece and Rome, and subsequently by its own religion, Christianity. As a supposed geo-cultural entity, Europe is the major focus of geography and history, which are taught as dominant subjects in schools, that is, when they are not dealing with the purely English, French or German varieties. The continent, like every old, and indeed new, nation, demands its exclusive history and geography, as we see from recent events in Africa where, after independence, the nations into which it was often illogically divided were defined, legitimized, in this very way. So too with Europe.

Right from ancient times, Europe has tended to be encapsulated, seen in opposition to Asia, a continent with its despotisms, its hydraulic civilizations, its inability to achieve capitalism, or even, according to some, to be as inventive as Europeans, who had their Christianity or their Protestant ethic, their entrepreneurship, their capitalism. According to some, it was always inherently backward. All this identification of Europe, Christianity and modernity has led to a neglect, even an implicit rejection, of the role of Islam in Europe. For example, one school of Spanish historians has seen the Muslim influences as being superficial, not touching

13

on the 'idiosyncratic nature' of the Iberians (Guichard 1994: 679).

The East, on the other hand, has been less certain of the boundary between the continents. The Levant used the expression *Ifranj* (Franks) to denote Europeans; only in the mid-nineteenth century did the term *Urūbā* (Europe) come into use. The term Franks excluded Europeans under Ottoman rule: in other words, it was not basically geographical but political. The more embracing notion of the West (*Gharb*) could include Russia and certainly the United States (Heyberger 2002: 2).

But Europe is not really even a geographic entity; it is separated from Asia only at one point, the Bosphorus, by a small stretch of water. North of that there is continuity over the Russian steppes, a complete terrestrial flow. I suggest that is also true of culture, and indeed of social organization. Indeed Europe has never been purely isolated, purely Christian.

Instead of a Christian Europe, one has to see the continent as penetrated by the three world religions (that is, written religions) that originated in the Near East and which indeed had a common mythology or sacred text; in order of arrival, these were Judaism, Christianity and Islam. And those religions took over from a set of moral beliefs and practices we designate in a negative, deprecatory, throw-away fashion as 'pagan' but which endured, even at a state or elite level, until the fifteenth century in Lithuania, and much later at a popular level – some have claimed throughout the Middle Ages in much of Europe.

Turning specifically to Islam, its advent should not be seen simply as usurping Christian Europe any more than the latter can be considered simply as the destroyer of the pagan or the scourge of the Jews. All have equal entitlements to be present, and in this general ('objective') sense none can be considered only as the Other; they are part of Europe, part of our heritage.

However, for Christian Europe, Islam was always the most formidable Other, ever since the eighth century. It is true that the other Other, the Jews, were physically nearer, since they lived dispersed as merchants and as refugees. As such they constituted a moral, a commercial, but never a politico-military threat, whereas Islam was not only the Other, but one that was apparently as powerful as the West in every sense. They had begun by invading Spain, reaching beyond the Pyrenees. Militarily they were as strong. Culturally too, constructing as they did the great Alhambra at Granada and the superb mosque at Cordoba and creating many other magnificent buildings on the soil of Europe. They brought with them important developments of the classical tradition which had been neglected in the West, in particular translations of the works of Aristotle, as well as advances that the Muslims themselves had made in the medieval sciences and in hygiene. Under Christianity, Roman baths fell into desuetude, as did their systems of water supply; indeed baths were at first often adversely associated with the ritual bathing of Judaism and the daily ablutions of Islam, as inimical to the Christian religion.

Part of those terrestrial flows have been represented in a constant movement of peoples, largely but not exclusively in an East–West direction. That has been so from prehistoric times, and historic ones too have been marked by the migration of Indo-Europeans, of Celts, of Ural-Altaic-speaking peoples such as the Finns, the Hungarians, and of course the Huns and others.

Culture too has often moved in the same way, first from the Near East to Europe, then in the reverse direction, but even where there has been no physical movement the boundaries have been open, so that much of culture has been shared. Culture has in fact moved both ways, as has conquest. Russia expanded in a swathe of territory stretching from the Black Sea to the Pacific; European culture ('modernization') and imperial rule have spread in the same direction. But earlier the movement was generally from East to West.

Of no sphere has this been clearer than religion, where the three main written creeds of the Near East, Judaism, Christianity and Islam, have pushed westwards (as well as

15

eastwards) along both shores of the Mediterranean, so that Islam, like Christianity and Judaism, is not simply a foreign religion but has long been established within Europe and has had a great influence not only on its politics but on its culture more generally. It is partly against the Jewish (and before that Phoenician) and Islamic elements that Europe, Western Europe, has defined itself as Christian. So that, in thinking of the role of Islam, we need to see it against the background of the transcontinental components in the history of East and West, and of their role in defining the latter, that is, of the Huns who operated in both regions, the Mongols who attacked China and the West at the same time, the Turks too, of whom Mao Tse-tung wrote in one of his Long March poems:

> Our forest of rifles darts ahead
> like the ancient Flying General
> who flew out of heaven to chase Turkish tribesmen
> out of Mongolia.[2]

The Orient, from which these world religions came, has always been of political interest to Europeans. The Greeks and then the Romans created major empires there, as did the Egyptians and the Persians. But with the advent of Christianity, the Orient, specifically Palestine, became the original source of the religion and an early centre of pilgrimage, just as Jerusalem and Mecca were to Jews and Muslims. Not only did people make arduous journeys to visit the Holy Land but there was early investment there. Access was rendered more difficult after the rise of Islam in the seventh century, and later attempts to 'free' the holy places, which the Muslims thought they had already 'freed', were of course one of the main, religiously inspired, motives of the Crusades, in which warriors were urged to their overseas duty by the popes and by the ecclesiastical establishment.

What I want to do is to consider firstly the extent, historically, of Islam's changing presence; it was always there as a point against which conceptually to define Christian identity in the East itself, as is very clear in the course of the Crusades, which constituted armed European invasions of Muslim territory. Secondly, I want to point to the major social and intellectual influences of Islam on Christian Europe, including the artistic impact. I touch upon its significance for Christian Europe's definition of itself, and more specifically the areas of confrontation or of difference. And finally, I look briefly at the role of Islam in contemporary Europe, especially its migrants from North Africa, the Near East and the Indian sub-continent.

The frequent neglect of the role of Islam in Europe (see López-Baralt 1994: 518; Guichard 1977; Torres and Macias 1998: 10), the emphasis on Christianity, in opposition to the Near East ('the Orient'), could be regarded as an aspect of the Orientalism which Edward Said, in his book of that name (1978), defines (outside the 'academic tradition') as 'a style of thought based upon an ontological and epistemological definition made between "the Orient" and (most of the time) "the Occident"' (1978: 2). Of course conceptually, as we have seen, that had long been the case ever since the Greeks opposed Europe and Asia, seeing the first as democratic, the second as autocratic, and differentiating them not only geographically but in other broad cultural terms. But there was another more concrete way in which the later Orient (by which Said means the Arab Near East) was inevitably not only differentiated from but dominated by the Occident economically, politically and militarily, though in earlier centuries the balance of power, culturally as well as politically, often went the other way.

In his introduction to *Orientalism*, Said wrote: 'The Orient is not only adjacent to Europe; it is also the place of Europe's greatest and richest and oldest colonies, its source of its civilizations and languages, its cultural contestant, and one of its deepest and most recurring images of the Other' (1978: 1). In addition, he notes, the Orient has helped to define Europe (or the West). The Eurasian landmass was divided on a lateral axis, East being distinguished from West and vice versa. However, Islam was not only a feature of the

Orient in a geographical sense; it came to Europe very early in its existence, with further profound implications for that continent. The Other in this sense was among us, not geographically separate, connected not only with European colonization, as Said suggests, but with the Islamic penetration ('colonization') of Europe. Islam was not only about what was happening in Damascus and Baghdad but, depending on the historical moment, in Barcelona, in Palermo, in Tirana, in Athens, in Budapest, in the Crimea and in Kiev and the Ukraine, as well as in Chechnya and Kosovo, to provide modern reminders of its extent.

Islam impinged upon Europe almost from its very beginning, in 622 CE, which was the year of the Hijrah ('the emigration', the 'severing of kinship ties'), when the faithful of Islam ('the surrender [to the will of God]'), that is the Muslims ('those who have surrendered'), followed Mohammed in leaving Mecca. There they had felt persecuted, and so established themselves in Medina, where a Jewish clan controlled the important market. From that base the prophet built up an alliance of clans which, from the early seventh century, were able to raid the rich caravans running between the Yemen, Mecca and Syria (Damascus and Gaza), trading in oriental goods from India and Ethiopia to the Mediterranean.[3] Both Mecca and Medina were major trading centres, the former having more political control, and were used by both Jewish and Christian merchants. Mohammed's first wife, for whom he had worked, was a trader, Khadijah, whose cousin Waraqah was a Christian.

Mohammed was in touch with both Judaism and Christianity, 'the people of the book' whose achievements were recognized, but under Islam they were nevertheless taxed (through the *jizya*, attempts to evade which encouraged conversion). But expansion from Arabia soon led to conflict with the Byzantine Empire, centred in the Eastern Christian capital of Constantinople. Islam had always had an important military side, being involved from the beginning in raids on the desert caravans. When Arabia was united under the Muslims, as a result of a series of alliances, towards the end of Mohammed's life (632 CE), by which time he was the strongest man in the country, the Muslim community, which had already raided Syria in 630, set out on a series of conquests, encouraged by the defeat of the Persian Empire by the Byzantine (627–8).

The expansion of that empire was phenomenal. Forty-six years after the flight of Mohammed from Mecca, his followers were under the walls of Constantinople. They attacked for seven summers but were defeated by the garrison using Greek fire and eventually retreated, with the loss, according to Gibbon, of some 30,000 men. A second siege (716–18) by way of the European side failed again through the fire-ships of the Greeks, although the making of such fire was said to have been invented by a Syrian engineer in the seventh century. In fact the fall of Constantinople had to wait seven centuries, until the coming of the Turks.

This move to the north, then to the west, to Spain by way of North Africa, later gave rise to the Crusades in the eastward direction, attempting to take back the Holy Land that Islam had conquered from the Byzantines. The second impact was of the Turks attacking that same Byzantine Empire to the north and moving into the Balkans before finally capturing its capital Constantinople, the Rome of the East, in 1453. Thirdly, yet farther to the north, were the invasions of the Mongol Tartars into Russia and Central Europe, beginning in 1237 with southern Russia, entering Poland and Hungary in 1241 in a two-pronged attack, but withdrawing on the death of the Great Khan.

The southern thrust

Unable to make headway against the Byzantine Empire, the Muslims thrust westwards. They arrived in North Africa well after the Jews and Christians, but appear to have been welcomed by the former, especially in Spain, since they had suffered discrimination in the latter stages of Visigothic rule when that kingdom adopted a form of Catholicism. The conquest of North Africa was rapid and resulted in the conversion of many Berber tribes. Historically, the territorial impact of Islam on Europe began in the south, where already within a hundred years of the Hijrah in 622 CE the Muslim forces, largely composed of Berbers, had reached the Atlantic and begun to cross into Spain by way of Gibraltar, and later to occupy the Mediterranean islands. The Arabs reached the Atlantic and Tariq ben Ziad crossed the straits of Gibraltar at the end of April 711, invited by an excluded branch of the local dynasty; on 19 July he defeated the Visigothic king, Roderick, and a month later siege was laid to Cordoba, where they were assisted by the Jewish community, who became the guards of the town and rejoiced at being linked to their co-religionists in the East, including Jerusalem itself. Under Islam the Jews and Christians had the status of *dhimma*, paying a special tribute but being granted an acknowledged position in the state. In this way they received a large measure of autonomy and suffered little anti-Semitism of the European variety (Zafrani 1996: 27). That situation permitted a great deal of commercial cooperation at all levels, as we see from the Geniza documents from Cairo. Much trade in Muslim lands, as in other spheres of public life, lay in the hands of the Jewish community. Such trade was facilitated by the fact that Islamic rule stretched from Spain to the Far East, permitting easy access to the long-distance trade, for example, in silks and spices from India and beyond.

This conquest of North Africa and the Arab domination of the Mediterranean had important consequences for Europe, and for centuries to come. In a famous thesis, Pirenne (1939) argued that Europe did not collapse with the fall of the Roman Empire in 400 CE but continued in much the same way as before, at least from the standpoint of trade, until 600. Then it was the appearance on the scene of the Muslims that disrupted commerce in the Mediterranean and led to an effective division between the Eastern and Western empires. The Merovingian kings in the north-west were isolated from the south but provided the early scaffolding of

the European Middle Ages, leading to the gradual emergence
of the Carolingian Empire. Without Mohammed, Charlemagne would have been inconceivable.

In a detailed examination of the archaeological and historical evidence for this thesis, Hodges and Whitehouse (1983)
argue that, while commercial life in the Mediterranean continued after Alaric's assault on Rome in 410 CE, it did so on
a diminishing scale; the metamorphosis from classical to
medieval had begun, with the construction of defensive hill-
top forts as against dispersed rural settlement in the plains.[4]
Warfare increased, as did taxes, so that 'the system gradually
wound down' (Hodges and Whitehouse 1983: 52). By the
time the Arabs arrived, the process was virtually complete.

So it was not the Islamic advance that made the great
difference. The Carolingians were already mainly cut off
from the Mediterranean, and the revival was based upon an
exploitation of the northern resources of the Rhine valley
and upon easy access to the North Sea in one direction and
to southern Germany in the other (Hodges and Whitehouse
1983: 171). The Carolingians intensified craft production,
especially in pottery, glass and querns, as well as developing
long-distance trade. A prime focus of this trade was the
Viking route (and hence included furs and slaves) from
the Baltic down the Volga and the long passage to Bulgar
and the Caspian Sea, leading straight to the centre of the
Abbasid Empire, near Baghdad. Already by 750 that empire
extended from Spain to Pakistan. By exchanging manufactured goods for silver coin, the Europeans obtained the
wealth needed to finance the Carolingian Renaissance. The
Umayyads were ousted from Damascus by the Abbasids
and some found refuge in Spain, where they took control of
Cordoba. The Abbasids moved away from the Mediterranean to Baghdad.

At this time Muslims in the Fertile Crescent were trading
with Africa, with India and with China, and artefacts originating from this trade route, which included a well-known
figure of Buddha, appear in the excavations of Scandinavian
cemeteries. So there was already a connection between the

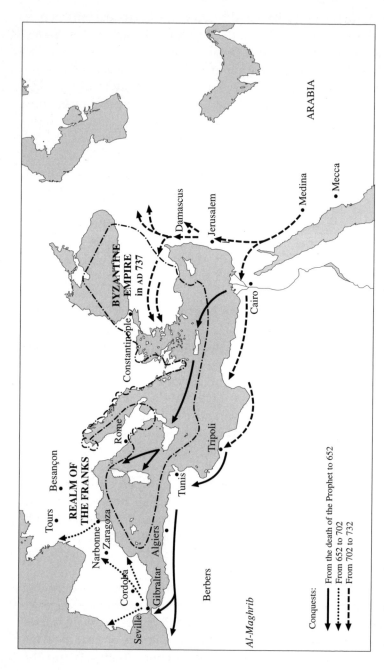

1.1 The Arab/Berber Invasions of Europe

rise of Islam and developments in Western Europe very soon after the birth of that religion. But there were also more direct connections. As we have seen, by 710, the Maghrib was conquered and Islam had reached the Atlantic Ocean. In that year, an Arab–Berber army had set out for and raided throughout the south of the Iberian peninsula, which they called al-Andalus (in 710 it was Vandalia).

The Muslim advance not only took over the Visigothic kingdom of Spain, but also captured some of its territories, at least temporarily, on the other side of the Pyrenees. Narbonne fell in 719 and was then subject to forty years of Muslim rule. The region of Septimania, consisting of the bishoprics of Narbonne, Nîmes, Agde, Béziers, Carcassonne, Maguelone (progenitor of Montpellier) and Elne, became a protectorate and possibly included a 'Jewish county' (in Septimania one-third of the landlords were Jewish). There were confrontations with the Franks based on Toulouse, although Aquitaine received the attention of the Muslim forces when they moved to attack the north. The Arabs also established themselves in southern France, from the north of the Garonne to the mouth of the Rhône. However, the Carolingian historian Paul the Deacon describes Muslims entering Gaul in about 720 as coming 'with their women and children to settle there' (Guichard 1994: 683). The daughter of the Duke of Aquitaine was given in marriage to a Muslim chief. The Muslim forces then proceeded to the gates of Tours and to the vineyards of Burgundy, including the towns of Lyons and Besançon. Had the march continued, muses Edward Gibbon, 'the interpretation of the Koran would now be taught in the schools of Oxford, and her pulpits might demonstrate to a circumcised people the sanctity and truth of the revelation of Mahomet' (Gibbon 1887: chapter 52, p. 88). In the north Muslims were apparently aiming to plunder the treasure that had accumulated at the shrine of St Martin in Tours and the bishop, St Galien, was said, in folklore, to have played some part in the Christian victory against the 'pagans'. However, in 732 Charles Martel defeated the invaders between Tours and Poitiers, the defeat of the Muslims (the additive 'hammer' he got through this victory) being widely welcomed throughout the Catholic world. He followed up his victory by putting Narbonne under siege six years later, an expedition that resulted in immense damage to the cities of the region and caused local feelings to be strongly anti-Frank. The campaign was later renewed by Charles's son, Pepin the Short, who pacified the local population and retook Narbonne from the Arabs in 759 (Saynes et al. 1986: 73–4).

While southern France was occupied only briefly by the 'Saracens', their constant presence in the eastern Mediterranean made a much more enduring impression. The coastal settlement of Maguelone, the site for the first cathedral of the area, was abandoned in favour of Montpellier, some kilometres to the interior. Place names continued to mark the whole littoral, a fortified village near Saint-Tropez, a pair of hills near Lodève (Gibre and Gibret), the record in the fifteenth century of a tenement called Peyra Sarrasina.[5] Scattered along the coast of southern France we find 'les tours Sarrasins' which, like the Martello towers of south-eastern England, remind one of ancient threats.

The activities of the Moors in Provence were the subject of an embassy from Otto the Great to the court at Cordoba, which he held responsible for their raids from the estuary of the Rhine to the Gulf of Saint-Tropez, leading to an exchange of visits from Cologne. Ambassadors also travelled between Constantinople and Cordoba, bringing gifts from the Basileus which included a Greek copy of a treaty on botany by Dioscorides, very important for the development of pharmacology in Andalusia. Ambassadors were already exchanged with European powers in 765 in the time of Pepin, father of Charlemagne, who had supported the Abbasid faction in Spain. Charlemagne himself sent an embassy there in 797 which was followed by a high-powered mission from the East that included the Governor of Egypt and brought a wide range of riches, notably a famous white elephant, a gift from the caliph, Harun al-Rashid. There was also a great deal of commercial exchange, giving rise to a large commercial and naval fleet in Muslim Spain, built in construction yards known as *dâr al-sina'a*, as the result of which the word 'arsenal' appeared in several European languages.

Large-scale conversion was not on the Muslim agenda; Christians were given rights as Mozarabs who had adopted the language and manners rather than the faith of the conquerors. They were an important element in Spanish society both before and after the conquest, especially round Toledo. At the beginning of the twelfth century Alfonso I of Aragon made a daring raid on Granada to liberate and resettle them in Christian lands. They had their own liturgy, which was suppressed as the result of the reforms of Pope Gregory VII (1073–85). Andalusia was an independent emirate (and later caliphate) ruled over by a member of the Syrian Umayyad dynasty (756–1031), who established themselves in Cordoba, declaring a caliphate in 929. The dynasty had been supplanted at the centre of Islamic rule in Baghdad by the Abbasids. The Umayyads ruled on much later in Andalusia, and it is through one of the Christian descendants, Maria de Padillo, that the British royal family has made a claim to be descended from the prophet.

The Umayyads were in many ways very successful, economically and politically, but a great liberation of written expression arrived in al-Andalus with the dissolution of the Umayyad dynasty into local kingdoms, *taifas*. These small courts modelled themselves on the caliphate at Cordoba and encouraged poets and writers in considerable numbers. The result was an efflorescence of Spanish Muslim culture in the eleventh century. That situation was to change with the advent of the reforming dynasty of Almoravids, Sanhajah Berbers originally from Senegal, and their yet more puritanical successors, also Berbers, the Almohads.

The invasions of the Almoravids and the Almohads were not purely military undertakings. There was a strong element of reform, of 'puritanism', of a return to the essentials of Maliki law, which had dominated the Maghrib. The rise of the Sufi brotherhoods was connected with a movement to modify the strict legal code on which reformers such as the Berber invaders had insisted, at least initially. These brotherhoods were becoming more common throughout the world of Islam, and the movement was particularly linked with the name of the jurist and theologian al-Ghazali (*d.* 1111), whose works enjoyed an immense success.

Previous conquerors of the Maghrib such as the Romans of North Africa had occupied the coast and exploited it for the benefit of their northern bases (especially for cereals). Now, in competition with Byzantines on the coast, the advancing Arabs spread inland into Berber territory. The Sanhajah Berbers extended as camel-herders across the Sahara, where they traded mined salt for gold, developing a caravan trade with the sub-Saharan black population, especially with the Kingdom of Ghana at Audagosht, where they had arrived around 990. After their leader had made a pilgrimage to Mecca in 1035, he and a Libyan teacher retreated, possibly to an island in the Senegal River, to practise a purer life. The founder of this movement was influenced towards Islamic reform by his encounter with the Libyan *faqih* at Kairouan in Tunisia, which no doubt motivated the movement to push northwards. But it was also fear of the northern caravan routes, on which their trade depended, becoming controlled by the Zenate Berbers.

The people of the retreat (the 'Marabous') founded the Almoravid dynasty (to use the Anglicized form) and declared a *jihad* against the 'impure' Sanhajah, thus beginning the conquest of Morocco, and even reaching Algiers. In 1086 they responded to a request for help from the Muslim rulers of Andalusia against the Christian forces to the north, who had recaptured Toledo. By 1110 all the petty Muslim states in Andalusia had come under Almoravid control and an African dynasty was now established in Europe. This dynasty was in turn condemned as impure by Ibn Tumart, another Berber from the Atlas, who had studied in Baghdad and Cairo, for using wine, playing musical instruments and not insisting upon the use of the veil in public. In 1125 with a small group of disciples he led a revolt against the ruling dynasty, and by 1147 the Almohads ('those who attest to the unity of God') had replaced the Almoravids in the Maghrib as well as in Andalusia.

Almohad rule was financially successful and undertook many public works; it built aqueducts for the big towns and extended the irrigated areas. The mulberry was encouraged because of the important silk industry around Granada. Ceramics, paper, craft work, weaving were the subject of international exchange, as well, of course, as cereals, vegetables and fruit. These commercial relations gave rise to continual embassies and correspondence, especially now that the Italians were becoming more involved in the Mediterranean trade. The regime was more 'puritanical' than its predecessors, whose monuments it sometimes destroyed. It was also responsible for the rejection of all animated figures in the art of Western Islam. When they captured Fez, they proceeded to whitewash 'the ornament, leaving the once ornate mosque bathed in an austere, white light' (Dodds 1994b: 612). At first they even used calligraphy sparingly on buildings. According to Mohammed, poetry was 'the Qur'an of Satan', the maker of pictures was cursed along with women who tattoo themselves, those who lived from usury, and sorcerers (Bürgel 1988: 11ff). Even learning was not altogether spared; while much of Islam welcomed and spread classical knowledge, some orthodox Jews and Muslims objected to 'Greek wisdom'. And, while the Muslims were normally hospitable to Jews, the puritanical Almohads tried to eliminate them from al-Andalus. But Almoravid strictures were partly countered by mystical elements such as occurred in Algeria.

The eventual fall of the Almohads was accompanied by the Christians' reconquest of the south, of Cordoba and Seville, leaving the last bastion of al-Andalus around Granada to endure another 250 years. In North Africa, various coastal towns such as Algiers and Oran became independent corsair republics, continuing the holy war in their attacks against the Christians, as the latter started to dominate the western Mediterranean. Those incursions led to Spanish reprisals and occupation, which in turn resulted in appeals to the Turks, whose intervention led to the end of an independent North Africa, apart from Morocco.

Spain was not the only point of entry into Europe. A further thrust towards Italy occurred in 912–13. The Shiite Fatimids in Tunisia, who were also expanding eastwards and later moved to Egypt, which was a major player in the Asian trade with India and China as well as with Africa, tried with limited success to expand into Europe from the Maghrib but only succeeded in making Sicily into a naval base. The Arab conquest of North Africa had long placed the Mediterranean islands in danger.

Maritime control in the Mediterranean depended upon having island bases. The Muslim threat to Christian shipping was greatest from the late eighth to the early eleventh century, when Islam held the chain of islands from Cyprus to the Balearics and had secured a toehold in southern Italy and southern France (Pryor 1988: 101). Islam won its first great victory at sea in 655, just after a raid on Cyprus. For the next thousand years it provided a challenge to Christian shipping along the valued Mediterranean route, the road to oriental luxuries. The Balearics, the key to the control of the western Mediterranean, were under Muslim control from 902 to 1229. Crete, which was the key to the eastern Mediterranean, was held between 824 and 961.

The island of Sicily was conquered by the Byzantines in 535 and finally lost to the Muslims in 902, though they had made their first landing in 652; it was always the Byzantine hope to recapture it. The Muslims had taken the island of Panteleria, south of Sicily, then in Byzantine hands, around 700, but did not mount a full-scale invasion of the main island until 827. In that year a small renegade force landed in Crete, which they took over from the Byzantines. At the invitation of a discredited Byzantine admiral, a large force was sent to Sicily, and Palermo fell in 831. The invasion of Sicily was mounted by the Aghlabid dynasty from Tangiers (Ifriqiya), and after a long struggle they gained control of the island and hence of the passage between the eastern and western Mediterranean. From here they crossed to the mainland and sacked Brindisi, Torrento, Adriatic ports, Sorrento, the Campania, even reaching Rome in 846. Those were raids. But in addition their assistance was called on by the Lombards of Benevento to take the town of Bari. For more than twenty years, from 847 to 871, Bari was the capital of a small, independent Islamic emirate. They attacked farther north, sacking St Peter's, then lying outside the walls of Rome, in 846, leading to a Carolingian offensive against the Arabs, but the latter still posed a threat to the Carolingians until 915. Naples and Salerno were constantly raided and the great monasteries of Monte Cassino and Volturno were looted. In 915 the Arabs were finally ousted and Christian trade in the Mediterranean began to revive (Hodges and Whitehouse 1983: 168).

The Fatimid ruler, Caliph al-Qua'im, sent his fleet to raid Genoa and the French coast (Terrasse 2001: 73). This activity caused the Byzantines to react and they too attacked, leaving Crete to call on the help of the Shiite Fatimids. The latter were unable to help but attacked western Sicily instead and captured Taormina, on the Italian mainland, in 963. As a result the Byzantines made a pact with the Fatimids, agreeing to their rule over Sicily and Calabria. Under the Muslims Sicily had been ruled first of all by the Aghlabids of Tunisia. After these adventures the Fatimids were ready to pursue their dream and conquer Abbasid Egypt. They took Egypt in 969, founding Cairo as their capital in 972.

Ten thousand Arabs, Berbers and Spanish Muslims were brought into Sicily, and eventually established their capital at Palermo. Under their rule, trade revived and that city became one of the greatest in the world (Finley et al. 1986: 52). The Arabs built mosques, gardens and palaces, resettled rural areas, renovating and extending the irrigation system, introducing new crops such as citrus, sugar cane, flax, cotton, silk, melons and date palms; with these products came the equipment and skills for processing them, especially cane mills and silk looms, which later came to play an important part in the 'modernization' of Europe and its colonies.[6] Taxation was rationalized, tolerance practised. Eventually they had to give up possession to the Normans, who captured Palermo in 1072. Apart from Muslim immigrants, there were many converts among the inhabitants (as happened in many places), leading to an Islamic majority in the population. But when the island was retaken by the Normans, no strangers to the area, beginning in 1060, it reverted to Christianity. The island of Malta followed the fate of Sicily, but the Arabs from Tunisia left that country their language, which became mixed with Sicilian Italian. After it was captured by the Normans, it was unsuccessfully besieged by the Turks in 1565, but the language remained even after the Christian reconquest. Culturally, dramatic expressions of the encounter between Muslims and Christians live on today in popular rituals, celebrating the encounter, as they do most prominently in Spain, especially at annual festivals and carnivals. But Muslim–Christian communication also flourished. The Cid fought for both sides; Jews and Muslims, as Mudejares, lived in Christian kingdoms. In Toledo, after the reconquest, Jews translated Arabic and Hebrew texts into Latin, then Spanish. The Muslim Mudejares were resettled in rural areas, where they carried out much of the work on irrigated lands for Christian overlords. Like the Jews they were at first allowed to practise their own religion, but were always subject to possible pogroms and suspected of encouraging the Turks to attack Spain to liberate them.

The tenth century saw the zenith of many Andalusian achievements. Granada became a great centre of silk production (Dickie 1994) as well as of other textiles. Its buildings included the Mosque of the Cotton Merchants. It was perhaps the biggest city in the whole of Europe and Africa. The town also profited from its fertile surroundings, irrigated with the Syrian water-wheels which provided two crops a year, as well as benefiting from the trans-Saharan trade in gold. Cordoba too became an intellectual centre and was described by a Saxon nun as the 'ornament of the world'. There the lute player Ziryab, from Baghdad, developed his school of music and 'civilized' both cuisine and tableware, as well as recommending crystal rather than jugs as a way of drinking special beverages, and introducing toothpaste.

One remarkable aspect over the whole history of Christian–Arab relations is the exchange of personnel through trade, through capture or through purchase. Female slaves from Europe became concubines of Muslim kings and princes, who sent singing-girls as gifts to the Christian rulers. In the Turkish case the Circassian slaves were acquired as concubines, and as such might become the mothers of rulers. The movement of concubines was largely a one-way trade because of the officially monogamous nature of Christian marriage and the reduced presence of slavery (but see Abulafia 1994, on Mallorca), and certainly singing-girls crossed the borders. Medieval romances tell of many romantic marriages between knights and warriors on one side and princesses on the other, in particular along the borderlands between the two faiths in Byzantium and Syria, as well as in Armenia, which constituted a Christian enclave within the Muslim lands. At that level the interchange was more bilateral and less common. Another main theme, closely connected with this exchange of personnel, is that of conversion (and, in the West, of the magical effects of baptism), as in the *Arabian Nights* with King Omar and Sophia, daughter of the King of Constantinople, who bears him a son.

El Cid Campeador was the Arabic name for lord, given to Rodrigo Diaz de Vivar (*d.* 1099), who was the vassal of Alfonso VI of Castile and León. He was forced into exile by court jealousies and he served the Muslim King of Saragossa. He later returned to the Christian ranks and became the protector of the King of Valencia, whom he defended against the Berber Almoravids when they had been called in from North Africa to help defeat the Christians. His exploits were celebrated in the *Poem of the Cid*, the first poem written in the Castilian language in the thirteenth century. He became the hero of Corneille's play *The Cid* (1637).

The Islamization of Portugal too began late in the first Muslim century. Between 710 and 732 Arab armies and their Berber followers crossed Iberia and invaded France, bringing with them a new flowering of Mediterranean civilization. Islam conquered the whole country except for some Christian chiefdoms in the far north. Otherwise the population was largely converted and young men left to work in the great Muslim cities. The wars of religion continued with the northern Christians raiding further and further south trying to dislodge the Muslims; their attempt was countered by the coming of the Almoravids from Africa. Nevertheless Henry of Burgundy established himself around Oporto and from there expanded his realm. The Algarve ('the West') was retaken after 1250; only later were Muslims expelled.

This was the time of the Crusades, which meant a movement in the opposite, eastward, direction. At the Council of Clairmont in 1095 Pope Urban II responded to an appeal from the Byzantine Empire for help against the Seljuq Turks, who had expanded into western Anatolia just as the Kipchak Turks in the Ukraine had cut off newly Christianized Russia from Byzantium.[7] The First Crusade, the holy war, began the next year and brought about the conquest of Jerusalem in 1099. The Christian *reconquista* of Spain was also under way, and scored its greatest victory to date at Toledo in 1085. The Crusades continued for more than 200 years, even though Jerusalem had already been retaken by the Muslims under Saladin in 1187. From then on the Europeans in Asia were confined to their massive coastal fortifications. But even after the Muslim victory at Hattin that year, which finally doomed the Kingdom of Jerusalem, the Saracens tolerated Christian pilgrims (palmers) visiting Jerusalem and other holy places, though the popes discouraged such visits as contributing to the enemy's exchequer (since the pilgrims had to pay a fee). Likewise Muslim merchants were forbidden to trade with non-Muslims, but that was an injunction that they, like the Christians, often overlooked; nevertheless there was less Muslim trade in Europe than vice versa (Constable 1994: 766).

The Crusades were abandoned but Europe continued to have her eyes on the Near East. Later on there were the more violent episodes of Napoleon's invasion of Egypt, which had some interesting consequences for knowledge systems even apart from the history of the Rosetta Stone and the founding of academic societies, as well as the British attack on the Suez area. And there were more peaceful invasions. The gathering of knowledge, as in visits such as Kingsley's (the author of *Eothen*, 1844) to the Holy Land, as in expeditions designed to capture antiquities, such as the Lion Gate of Babylon, for European museums, became dominant ways in which the West now came to penetrate the East. Archaeology, linguistics, history, anthropology, not to speak of the incessant search for oil to fuel the internal combustion engine, all added to the East's sense of exploitation by the West.

The influence of the Crusades has been much disputed. Prutz (1883) saw their historical and cultural significance as unsurpassed, with Frankish knights opening up the wonders of the East to astonished Europeans. That was a judgement revised by Runciman (1969), who saw the episode as costing Europe a few million men without bringing any enlightenment, and as involving the last barbarian invasions of Constantinople (1204) (Metlitzki 1997: 4). What they developed was a general aspiration to copy the comforts of the East.

So, while many major political relations between the Christian and Islamic worlds were defined by opposition, indeed by conflict, taking the form of the 'holy war', either in the Crusade or in the *jihad*, led by the Cross or by the Crescent, there was inevitably an interpenetration of the populations through trade and proximity (and certainly of cultural communication). Above all the conflicts gave rise to captives on both sides. The Crusades produced many prisoners, the better-off of whom were subject to ransom, as in the case of Richard, Coeur de Lion (the Christians' answer to Saladin, widely celebrated in Western Europe, as in the pub sign of the Saracen's Head). The poorer sort of prisoners had to make their own arrangements with their Muslim overlords. When the Crusaders did establish themselves in their coastal fortifications of Syria, they necessarily had to interact with the local population for the supply of food and services.

They also took advantage of their opponents' superior skills in medicine and hygiene. Some of the earlier invaders married Arab Muslims and adopted many of their customs. The Templars in particular developed close relations with Islam, which was one of the reasons for their suppression in 1318. And other orders made Palestine their home, seizing back the holy places from the infidel. They even transformed those places in their imagination. Among the Crusaders' myths was that the Dome of the Rock was the biblical Holy of Holies and the al-Aqsa Mosque the Palace of Solomon (Howard 2000: 181).

Andalusia had to wait for Christian rule until the reconquest of Granada took place in 1492. The Moors of that town were at first granted religious freedom, as was usual when a town surrendered on 'terms', but later the introduction of forced mass conversions led to a revolt in 1499–1500 and again in 1568; after their defeat three years later they were given the choice of conversion or expulsion. Many Moors accepted conversion, but the Morisco community that resulted was never fully accepted by the Christians. Later under Philip II some of their lands were confiscated, and in 1567 a decree forbade their use of Moorish names and clothing as well as of the Arabic language. Their customs and ceremonies were forbidden, their cemeteries were closed and even the use of their baths proscribed (for fear of these being interpreted as ritual ablutions) – indeed the beautiful Alhambra baths were removed altogether. Christians too were forbidden to use them (De Castro 2002: 204). The Moriscos were also forbidden to observe Muslim taboos on pork as well as the eating of couscous (De Castro 2002: 207). However, in the privacy of their own kitchens they continued 'to eat as Moriscos', and indeed some of their practices were taken up by Castilians. As a result of these prohibitions the Moriscos were in a state of revolt and sought help from the Turks and North Africa. After two years the uprising was defeated and the inhabitants were scattered throughout Spain and yet further afield.[8] Meanwhile, the community sent an envoy to Mameluk Egypt, not to ask

34

them to invade, but at least to threaten reprisals against Christians living in the East. Spain then became concerned and Ferdinand sent a special ambassador, Peter Martyr, to dissuade the Mameluk ruler from taking any action. When help was refused, the Moriscos approached the Ottoman court under Bajazet II, but with the same result. However, the Turks had been made conscious of the plight of their fellow Muslims, and their subsequent ventures in the eastern Mediterranean, including their defeat at Lepanto, were perhaps prompted by the earlier appeals. However, that did nothing to prevent the expulsion of all the Moriscos in 1609.

After the reconquest, Muslims remained numerous, not only in Andalusia but in Valencia, where they formed a large peasant population subject for 300 years to a land-owning nobility who protected them as good taxpayers and as improvers of the land. 'In spirit, Morisco Valencia remained part of Islam, . . . a nation within a nation, with its own leaders' (Lynch 1965: 208). Moreover, the Muslims formed a growing percentage of the population, the remainder of which feared their numerical dominance. Indeed the very size of the Muslim community was one of the main reasons for its expulsion in 1609.

After 1492 the commercial relations of Christian Europe with Mediterranean ports (and even Norway in 1262–3, according to Colley 2002: 229) were strong, with Marseilles selling wine in Tunis and Montpellier and Narbonne being actively engaged (Colley 2002: 228). The Europeans became stronger and stronger in the Mediterranean, especially with the Normans establishing themselves in Sicily and demanding tribute from Tunisia until al-Mustansir refused in 1266, when Charles of Anjou became king. A number of treaties guaranteed access for Christians to North African ports, where they possessed 'factories' (*funduq*). On the Muslim side, there was also an important Christian militia of the Hafsides that included renegades and captives, who played a significant role in the history of the Maghrib.

North Africa generally had sufficient wheat to feed itself and it also exported to al-Andalus, whose population was swollen by refugees. Morocco also had a surplus of olives, dates and cane sugar for exchange. In addition the country exported leather as well as fine merino wool, especially to Genoa. From at least the tenth century Granada had culti- vated the production of silk, which again was exported to Europe, until Italian silk later took over.

Under the new dispensation, the Muslims lived on mainly as forced converts, as New Christians or Moriscos. This policy, initiated in Castile in 1502 when the Muslims were given the choice of conversion or expulsion, was as we have seen partly the result of fear of the Ottoman Turks (Lynch 1965: 206), who were now making their presence felt in the eastern Mediterranean. For Spain was still being raided from the Maghrib, as a result of which Moriscos were forbidden access to maritime districts. A similar fate was suffered by the Jews, who were expelled very shortly after the capture of Granada. Later on, in 1609, even converted Muslims suffered the same fate. At that time Spain saw itself as constantly threatened by the Turks not only on the Mediter- ranean front but also in Central Europe. But there was also a strong ideological element. The Inquisition started up in 1478, the Jews were expelled in 1492 (the year of Columbus's voyage to the Americas), the Muslims followed in 1609 (they were essential to the rural economy of Spain). When this happened, the decline of Spain set in, despite the profits from the Americas.

The Islamic invasion of North Africa had led to the con- version of the vast majority of the population. Jews remained throughout the Maghrib and often felt themselves better treated than by the Christians. As a result, while many came to Spain with the Muslims, many returned to North Africa when they were expelled. And in Spain, as everywhere throughout the Mediterranean, there were many converts. With the reconquest the Spanish rulers were caught in a cleft stick. In the first place the Muslim peasantry were essential to the working of agriculture, because of their knowledge of irrigated farming and because of their very numbers. On the other hand there was the religious struggle against the Moors, which undoubtedly had much popular support – as we see from the long tradition of folk plays on the battles between Christians and Moors performed at festival times.

Apart from peoples and the religions, inventions and knowledge of Asian origins spread through Europe by way of the Muslims, especially to Spain, which during unsettled times in the Near East became a haven for Muslim and Jewish scholars. These I discuss later under the heading of cultural influences.

The middle way

Apart from the Arabs in the Mediterranean, there were the Turks, who constituted the second major thrust of Islam, that is, of the Seljuqs, and then the neo-Mongols, who migrated continuously from Central Asia between 1055 and 1405. The Seljuqs were converted to Sunni Islam probably by Sufi missionaries after the beginning of the eleventh century. They conquered Khorasan (Persia), then Baghdad in 1055 and moved on to Syria, encountering some Byzantine resistance in the Armenian highlands. The Ottoman Turks were a conglomerate tribe formed in Anatolia, who made their capital at Bursa, near Constantinople, in 1326. They crossed into European Thrace at the service of rival factions in Constantinople, occupying Byzantine territory and establishing a second capital at Edirne on the European side. They were militantly Muslim and spread into Greece and the Balkans before entering Constantinople in 1453 under Mehmed II.

One of the myths of the Renaissance is to attribute the revival of learning to the Greeks who fled the eastern Mediterranean at that time. The Turks were envisaged as despots by Marlowe, Racine and others, in confirmation of the long-established notion of oriental despotism. But that did not stop communication. Ambassadors travelled in both directions, as did merchants. European artists paid visits. Gentile Bellini was invited to Istanbul by the sultan to paint his portrait. Other influences were present (Jardine and Brotton

2000). The sultan, Mehmed, was a Renaissance man himself, and one of his favourite writers was Livy, read to him by an Italian, Cyriac of Ancona (Burke 1998: 58). But the Turks were also a great threat and seen as such. Giovio, who wrote a book about the Ottoman Empire, did so to encourage a crusade against the Turks (Burke 1998: 210).

On the European mainland the Turks first established themselves at Gallipoli in 1354, taking Adrianople in 1362, from where they moved up the Maritsa valley into the Balkans. They conquered Bulgaria and a substantial part of the Greek peninsula. Serbia was overrun in 1398 and Wallachia was made a tributary. Hungary and the Hapsburg possessions were subject to occasional attack; they suffered a bad defeat at Nicopolis in 1396 but were relieved by the attack on the Turks by Tamerlaine and his Mongols at Angora in 1402. They then turned their attention to the Mediterranean. But, with the fall of Constantinople, the Turkish armies consolidated their holdings on the Balkan peninsula, heralding the end of Hungarian influence in that area. By 1417 they had established themselves in the market town of Gyirokastra in Albania, on the route from Greece to Central Europe, where they had many converts from Christianity and built an imposing fortress and many merchants' houses. The Ottoman Empire attacked the unified states of the Jagiellonian dynasty of Poland, conquering the commercial trading cities of Kaffa (1475) and Kilia and Akkerman (1484), a move that completely cut off Polish trade with the Orient. Poland was also attacked by the Tartars of Crimea, who had come under Ottoman rule in 1475 and who made raids for slaves and booty into Red Ruthenia and Little Poland. The Tartars reached Krakov in 1498–9 as well as Moldavia. Tsar Ivan III even allied himself with the Crimean Turks to attack his neighbour Lithuania at the end of the fifteenth and beginning of the sixteenth century.

It was Suleiman the Magnificent who renewed the attack against south-western Europe. Belgrade, the fortress on the Danube, collapsed in 1521. Rhodes, Christianity's main stronghold in the eastern Mediterranean, fell in the following

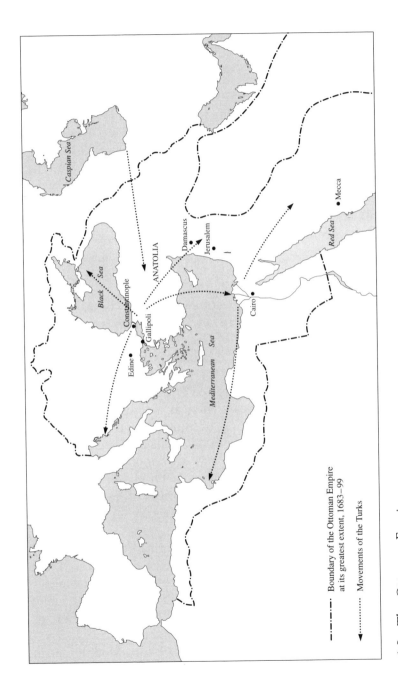

Caspian Sea

Black Sea

Constantinople

Edine •

Gallipoli

ANATOLIA

Damascus •

Jerusalem •

Cairo •

Mediterranean Sea

Red Sea

Mecca •

— · — · — Boundary of the Ottoman Empire
at its greatest extent, 1683–99

··········▶ Movements of the Turks

1.2 The Ottoman Empire

year. The Mediterranean world became alarmed. Even so the Protestants were reluctant to aid the Hapsburgs in their struggles against the Turks, without concessions being granted regarding the Catholics in Germany. The situation was brought to a climax when in 1529 the Austrian ruler provoked the Turks into attacking (Fischer-Galati 1959: 36). The consequent siege of Vienna was not part of a Turkish plan to invade Germany but was intended to serve as a warning to the Hapsburgs against interference in Hungary, where the Porte were supporting an alternative ruler. Nevertheless the move aroused the leaders of contemporary Europe at least to talk about mounting a crusade. By and large public opinion favoured non-intervention,[9] but the Emperor Charles V called a Diet at Augsburg in 1530 both to consider religious 'errors' and to 'alleviate the evils which were feared on the part of the Turk' (Fischer-Galati 1959: 42).

The conquerors, who eventually seized control of the islands of Crete and Cyprus and of the Morea, continued their raiding until the fall of Constantinople, one hundred years later. Following that the Balkans were to be dominated by the Turks for the next five centuries. Belgrade was captured in 1521, Hungary defeated at Mohács Field in 1526, Vienna besieged three years later, as a result of which the Turks gained control of most of Hungary and Transylvania, as well as of the principalities of Wallachia and Moldavia. They retained their rulership, at least nominally, of much of the Balkans until the Congress of Berlin in 1878.

The memory of the Turkish investment of Eastern Europe remains strong in nations such as Hungary and Serbia. For the first, the name of Mohács Field, where many Hungarians were killed, lives on. So too in Serbia does the Field of the Blackbirds in Kosovo. But in Western Europe the threat has had less importance. Indeed, before the defeat of Mohács Field, the Hungarians found it difficult to interest Germany and Austria in coming to their aid. Spain was different, having only recently reconquered Andalusia in 1492.

The Turkish fleet appeared in the western Mediterranean in the late 1520s when incursions were made into Spanish territorial waters. The sultan would not forgive Spain's humiliation of the Moors. In 1529 the corsair Barbarossa raided Algiers. The Ottomans were receiving support from the French under Francis I, but Barbarossa was appointed admiral of the Spanish fleet in 1534 and ordered to seize Tunis. He ravaged the coasts of Sicily and southern Italy. But a counter-attack was mounted by the Emperor Charles V, who reconquered Tunis and defeated Barbarossa, victories which were countered in their turn by the French, who stimulated Turkish action in the form of new raids in the Mediterranean and incursions into Slovenia and Croatia.

There had already been a number of major clashes between Turks and Christians in the Mediterranean, which was largely at the mercy of North African corsairs and of the Turkish fleet. The corsairs had been pushed by the nature of the country, in Tripoli for example, to live off the sea rather than the land. As a result they threatened Spanish grain supplies from Sicily; from 1560 onwards they raided everywhere. Even Western Europe was conscious of their presence, with North Africans raiding, and sometimes trading, as far as the coasts of Britain. Philip II intended to attack Tripoli that same year but went for Djerba instead. Here he was disastrously defeated by the Turkish fleet. As a result, he decided to re-arm and to join an alliance with Venice and the papacy to defeat the Turks, who had become a yet greater threat by capturing Cyprus from Venice in 1571, which then lost access to its resources of sugar, salt, cotton, copper and wine.

In the early modern period knowledge of the East is said to have been transmitted through Venice, 'the eye of all the West'. For centuries she had been Europe's main link with the Levant when the Mediterranean became an Islamic lake, and she continued to trade with the East. So Venice was always a doubtful ally of Spain, being dependent upon grain supplies from southern Russia and the Balkans, all of which had to come through the Turkish-controlled Bosphorus. She could trade through the eastern Mediterranean only with Turkish approval. Nevertheless, on this occasion Venice contributed well-armed galleys to the joint fleet which in 1570 famously defeated the Turks in the Gulf of Lepanto, putting a temporary end to the naval threat from the East. But within three years the Turks had recovered sufficiently to score a notable victory against Spain at Tunis. That victory led to a *détente* if not a formal truce in the Mediterranean that enabled Philip to turn to Northern Europe, where he was engaged in a constant armed struggle in the largely Protestant Low Countries.

The Turks were fighting on more than one front, also attacking Austria-Hungary. Protestant England too posed problems for Spain as, freed from the papal bans, it was courting the Muslim powers not only in Turkey[10] but in Morocco, where Elizabeth's technical assistance helped that country to mount a trans-Saharan expedition to conquer the Niger Bend. She sold weapons to the Moroccans in the late sixteenth century to use against the Catholic Portuguese. But it was not only reasons of state that led to these alliances. Islam was seen as closer to Protestantism in banning images from places of worship, in not treating marriage as a sacrament and in rejecting monastic orders (Colley 2002: 122). When Elizabeth sought an alliance with the Turks, the argument was used that Protestants and Muslims were alike haters of the 'idolatries' practised by the King of Spain, an interesting example where the hatred of icons was seen to bring together Muslims and the Reformed Church. Her attitude represented wider views among Protestants. Luther rejected war against the Turks as being un-Christian (Fischer-Galati 1959: 8): the attacks of the infidel on Europe represented God's punishment for sinfulness and for the wickedness of the Antichrist, the pope. Of course political factors were also involved. Long before this period, in about 1212, a rumour circulated against King John that he had tried to make an alliance with Morocco in order to outflank France. That was a continuing possibility. In this case Elizabeth wanted the sultan to attack Spain as a diversionary blow in order to hold up the preparations he was making against England for the Armada.[11]

The desire for alliance was not all on one side. The predicament of the Moriscos meant the Turks were as keen to negotiate for Protestant help against the Catholics (in this case, Spain) as the Protestants were to ally themselves to the Muslims. The Moriscos were encouraged by Elizabeth, who gave military help to Morocco, where many of them had withdrawn. Indeed the town of Sallee was largely occupied by them, and their forces took part in the campaign of the Moroccan ruler, al-Mansur, to cross the Sahara and defeat the Songhai kingdom, seizing quantities of gold to help him pursue his plans. When Elizabeth died, her successor, James I, a great believer in divine right, was dismayed at the idea of encouraging rebellion, especially of the 'infidel', and he cancelled earlier understandings. But Charles I sought Moroccan aid against Spain in the 1620s, and from 1704 onwards Britain relied on Algiers and Morocco to provision Gibraltar and Malta.

By the Elizabethan period the crusading spirit had largely died down, but there developed an important commerce with Muslims in the Mediterranean, partly in woollen goods but also in weapons. The Muslims in turn exported sugar and fruit to Britain. Nor was it only in commerce that contacts were made; raiding continued. Muslim ships sailed into the Channel and round the coasts, in an attempt to capture both goods and men. In the 1630s, Algerian corsairs attacked coastal villages in western England and Ireland, and at the same time Morocco dispatched its first large-scale embassy to London to negotiate ransom for its captives taken by the English (Colley 2002: 115). Between 1600 and the early 1640s North African corsairs seized more than 800 British trading vessels in the Mediterranean and the Atlantic, possibly capturing around 12,000 subjects. The British made similar attacks, but even more intensively, in the Mediterranean, acting much as Muslim corsairs. In the course of these conflicts many men were captured, especially Britons, some of whom were ransomed, some settling in North Africa, others reduced to slavery or to working for the enemy. Interest in Islam developed at the same time. That was the period that saw the establishment of the first chair in Arabic at Oxford and Cambridge.

The sixteenth century produced greater diplomatic efforts and a lively series of missions and exchanges with the Muslim powers, in particular Turkey. The sultan received expensive gifts from the European powers, not only from the Protestants but from the Catholics as well. Ambassadors as well as others from the East visited the West. While the crusading spirit had lingered and was replaced with a desire to trade, the fear of an Islamic attack, lower in Western Europe, persisted in the Mediterranean. Conflict still continued. As we have seen, when James VI came to the English throne, he reversed Elizabeth's policy and made peace with Spain. Swift retaliation against shipping followed. Between 1610 and the 1630s, Devon and Cornwall lost a fifth of their shipping to North African corsairs. In 1625 alone, nearly one thousand seafarers from Plymouth were seized, most within 30 miles of the shore (Colley 2002: 49). Such depredations led to resentment against the government, and Charles I had to levy the controversial ship money to improve the navy relative to the corsairs.

At the same time Muslims also played a major role in literature. In England we have Marlowe's *Tamburlaine* and Shakespeare's *Othello* ('the Moor of Venice'), together with a host of other plays of the same period. In France, Racine's *Bajazet* became a classic. In Spain, it was tales of the reconquest that figured in literature, especially of the Cid. There we also have popular expressions of the conflict between Christians and Moors. In England the River Thames saw highly elaborated re-enactments of sea battles between Christian and Muslim forces (Matar 1999: 145). In those Jacobean pageants, the Cross (of St George) was victorious over the Crescent. The Elizabethan period did not see an end to the portrayal of Muslims on stage. In 1751 the Covent Garden Theatre staged a re-enactment of 'a matter of Barbary' in the form of displaying men in rags and clanking chains as in their captivity in North Africa, from which they had just been released.

Let us return to Central Europe. The powers of the Porte meant that it was a constant element in European politics over the centuries, more significant after the fall of Constantinople than either Arab or Mongol Islam. Turkey was also a potential factor in internal politics because, while one party might win the support of other Christian powers, the other might seek the help of Istanbul. In Hungary the Hapsburg Staathalter Ferdinand had himself proclaimed ruler, and at the same time another claimant, Zápolya, secured Ottoman support for the same purpose. When the Emperor Charles V failed to agree with the Protestants in 1539, he sought a truce with the Ottomans. So at a different time did Ferdinand, and certainly Francis I of France tried to do so in opposition to the emperor, while Queen Elizabeth of England sent an ambassador to arrange an alliance against the Catholic powers. In Germany the necessity of raising funds to combat the threat of a Turkish attack on Vienna and beyond meant that the Lutherans had the possibility of forcing concessions from the emperor in respect of the Catholics. In this way, the politics of the Austro-Hungarian Empire was clearly influenced by Muslim (Turkish) pressures right up to the eighteenth century. The Reformation was a threat to the unity of the Austro-Hungarian Empire and therefore of its capacity to resist. There was a certain collusion of Protestants with Islam, and it was largely the Catholic forces that resisted the Islamic advance.

The struggle of the Protestants for recognition in Germany after 1521 ended in 1555 with their triumph at the Diet of Augsburg. They triumphed largely because of the external threats to the Hapsburg hegemony in Europe from the French under Francis I in the West and from the Ottomans in the East. In the East the problem centred on the state of Hungary, coveted by both sides and subject to frequent Turkish invasions. Indeed it has been remarked that 'the consolidation, expansion and legitimizing of Lutheranism in Germany by 1555 should be attributed to Ottoman imperialism more than to any other single factor' (Fischer-Galati 1959: 117).

45

The Ottomans continued to move westwards against Christians in the Balkans and in Hungary, reaching the outskirts of Vienna in 1683 during the course of a war with Austria and Poland (1682–99), in which they eventually suffered defeat at the Battle of Zenta (1698). After the Treaty of Carlowitz at the end of the war (1699) between the Ottoman Empire and the 'Holy League', the counter-attack began as a result of which Austria gained control of most of Hungary, Transylvania, Croatia and Slovenia, while Venice took Dalmatia and the Morea, and Poland won Podolia. Russian advances against the Ottomans began under Peter the Great at about the same time, at the end of the seventeenth century. That pressure was continued by Catherine, who gained the lands north of the Black Sea up to the Dnestr River. By a treaty of 1774, Russia not only acquired territory in the region of the Black Sea but also claimed to have become the protector of Orthodox Christians throughout the Turkish Empire, a claim with important historical and cultural consequences. Russia and Austria then continued to participate in the dismemberment of that empire in Europe, so that in 1812 Bessarabia went to Russia. However, at the end of the Napoleonic War, Turkey regained control of some of the Balkans. Subsequently the process of dismemberment continued, leading eventually to the Crimean War (1853–6), in which the Western powers tried to prop up Turkey against Russia. In 1878, after the defeat of Turkey by Russia, the Treaty of San Stefano defined a new dispensation for the Balkans, giving independence to Bulgaria, Serbia, Montenegro and Romania, but that had to be revised under Western pressure at the Congress of Berlin in the same year. Eventually, as the result of the defeat by the Balkan alliance in 1911–12, the Ottomans lost all their territories in Europe, except for a strip round Constantinople. It is that strip that now gives them a claim to a European as well as an Asian identity; their admittance to the European Union would bring a large Muslim power into the predominantly Christian conclave.

Under Turkish rule Christians in all these territories, known collectively as Rum (derived from Rumelia, or Rome), had supplied recruits, slaves of a kind (*devsirme*), by which one in four boys was trained in Istanbul to become a senior administrator. The Albanians were distinguished from the rest of the Balkan populations not only by their non-Slavic language but also by a large-scale conversion to Islam under the Turks in the fifteenth century (though some mountain clans became Catholic). The rest of the Balkans was either Greek Orthodox or mixed. So the defeat of the Turks at Vienna was the beginning of their retreat from Europe. That led to their withdrawal from Greece with the War of Independence of 1821 (in which the poet Byron became a hero), from Bulgaria with the advance of the Russians in the war of 1877–8 and elsewhere in the Balkans before the First World War. With Greece there was an exchange of populations, an ethnic cleansing, whereby with few exceptions Muslims went from Greece to Turkey and Christians from Turkey to Greece. But elsewhere, in Albania, Kosovo, Bosnia-Herzegovina, and parts of Macedonia and Bulgaria (with its settlers of Tartar and Circassian origin), Muslims remain until today.

The time of the greatest pressure on Europe from Turkish Islam came during the period of the Renaissance and the Reformation, beginning early in the sixteenth century. What were the connections between the Turkish advance and the important developments in Europe? The resurgence of interest in Greek was much encouraged by the Council of the Roman and Greek Orthodox Churches held in Ferrara and then Florence in 1438, which was a direct consequence of Turkish pressure. The attempt to unify the churches, spurred on by the need of the Eastern Emperor, John Paleologus, for help against the Turks then threatening Constantinople, failed, but the presence of so many Greek scholars included in the 700-strong delegation stimulated 'the quickening interest in classical texts and classical history, in classical art and philosophy, and particularly the study of Plato, that great hero of the humanists' (Hibbert 1979: 68). Some stayed in Florence, where Cosimo Medici attended lectures on Plato and started an academy for Platonic studies, as well as building up his amazing library of some ten thousand codices of Latin and Greek authors.

There is a sense in which the Renaissance can be seen as a reaction to the splendours of the Islamic East. That had provided models of luxury and civilization, including a deeper knowledge of classical texts. The return to those texts, whether they came through Spain or Constantinople, was at one level an appeal to the past in the face of the Ottoman and Mongol societies that had penetrated Eastern Europe and that were being opposed by the Orthodox and Catholic churches, the churches of the East and West Roman empires respectively. The return of the classical past emphasized European achievements in Ancient Greece and Rome, playing down the Near East with its Christian and Jewish roots and its Islamic presence. Indeed the return to the classical world was seen as the answer to the threat from Islam to European culture. George Sarton commented that the humanists' love of Greece and Rome was nourished by their hatred of Islam. To counter the culture of the Arabic world, the revival of antiquity was carried forth on many fronts. He wrote that the Renaissance was 'partly a reaction against influences (especially those represented by Avicenna and Averroës). The anti-Arabic drive was in full swing in Petrarch's time' (Stimson 1962: 103).

The classical world provided a new model for a future which modified the religious by the secular, seeking to give the former a more restricted role and to allow a greater one for other forms of knowledge and action. The appeal to the classics made it easier to circumvent the picture of the world derived from religious texts and to open the way to Galileo, to Bacon, to the Scientific Revolution leading through the Enlightenment to Newton, to Darwin and to the prevailing domination of secular thinking. A humanistic and scientific view of the world had also been present in Islam at some stages in its history, and their *madrasa* education, at its highest level, was not confined to the religious alone. Muslims too had their dissidents and their heretics. Indirectly both the classical revival and the Scientific Revolution owed something to Islam, in which those traditions had been partly preserved. The Renaissance was made possible through the translations from the Greek, partly by way of Arabic (López-Baralt 1994: 509).

The Reformation provided stronger and more positive links with the Muslim East. There were commercial, political and ideological links between the Protestants and the Turks. Catholic rulers such as Francis I were also in touch with Constantinople, sending lavish presents to the sultan (Jardine and Brotton 2000), but the Protestants did not see themselves as bound by papal bans on trading with the enemy, nor did they recognize the division of the world decreed by the Vatican. In West Africa, Dane guns, manufactured and traded by the Protestant powers, were sold to the Muslims and to other enemy forces. In fact part of the success of the Protestant countries of Holland, Britain, north Germany and Scandinavia in penetrating the markets opened up by Spain and Portugal lay precisely in their being freer to establish commercial and other relationships with Muslim and pagan regimes.

The northern entry

The movement of the Tartars to the Ukraine was the third of the major thrusts of Islam and, like the previous thrust, it has also to be seen as part of a millennia-old stream of Ural-Altaic and Turkic-speaking peoples coming into Europe from the steppes of Central Asia, a movement which had had such dramatic repercussions on the Roman Empire, an empire, at least in a Christian form, that partly recovered. When the Mongols arrived in Europe, the Arabs were already present in Russia, having defeated the Turkic Khazars in 661, and in the Caucasus in 737, when their capital was destroyed. About three years later the Khazars adopted Judaism. That was two centuries before the state of Kiev converted to Christianity, in 988. Turkish nomads, later the Kipchaks, who were not at that time Muslims, penetrated the southern steppe of Russia in the eleventh century, and were followed by Muslim merchants into the towns of the Crimea and the Upper Volga. Those earlier movements westwards across the steppes were followed by that of the Mongols and the Golden Horde under the Great Khan, who reached the now Christian Kiev in 1223, defeating the hetero-geneous alliance of princes on the Kalka River.

The Mongol Empire had been created by Genghis Khan, who received his title of ruler in 1206. His first main target was China to the south, but he was led into an attack to the west after some of his envoys who had been dispatched in that direction were executed. In revenge his forces set off through Afghanistan and continued until they crossed the Caucasus in 1223, defeating a Russo-Kipchak force that year. But due to the death of Genghis in 1227 they did not invade Eastern Europe until the winter of 1236–7, led by Batu, the grandson of Genghis Khan, who founded the Khanate of Kipchak, and was elected as the commander-in-chief of the western part of the Mongol Empire. By 1240, the year in which he sacked Kiev, Russia's greatest city, he had conquered all of Russia, then in 1241 defeated a Silesian army (from an area now in Poland) and a Hungarian force two days later. About to invade Western Europe, he heard of the death of the head of the empire and retreated with his forces to take part in the next election. The state he established in southern Russia was ruled by his successors for the next 200 years. Obviously the Golden Horde became a major factor in European politics, especially after converting to Islam under Ghazan (1295–1304), although Islamization had already begun under Berke (1257–67), that is, not long after the fall of Kiev, a conversion that associated the state with the Iranian tradition. The new conquerors established a rule that at its high point included the Crimea, the Polovtsian steppe from the Danube to the Ural River, Moldavia and parts of Siberia, as well as territories in Asia. These Tartars were in contact with Timur (the Tamburlaine celebrated by Christopher Marlowe), who aided them in enabling a threat to be made against Moscow, but in the end Timur set about attacking the Tartars themselves, probably wanting to establish his own control of the East–West routes.

The Cossacks, whose name derives from the Turkish *kazak*, meaning an adventurer or free man, lived in the northern highlands around the Black and Caspian seas. In the fifteenth century the term originally applied to semi-independent Tartar groups found in the Dnepr region (as well as to the fleeing serfs in that area) who established self-governing military communities which eventually received privileges from the Russian government in return for recognized military services. That was also the case in sixteenth-century Poland. It was the Cossacks who led the early colonization of Siberia under the Russian umbrella.

The Golden Horde passed westwards as far as Lithuania and Poland on the Baltic coast, ruling much of that area between 1241 and 1242, defeating the Polish army at the Battle of Chmielnik and the Siberian knights of the Teutonic Order at Legnica. In 1242 they returned to Mongolia to elect a new khan, but for another fifty years remained masters of Red Ruthenia, east of Little Poland, with its headquarters at Krakov. By 1240 the indigenous pagan Lithuanian tribes had been moulded by Duke Mindayas into a state which accepted Christianity around 1251, though general conversion did not take effect for another hundred years or so. Nevertheless the country was able to resist the attempts of the Teutonic knights from Prussia to take over the whole of the Baltic area. Before Lithuania became Christian the Lithuanian people were even labelled 'Saracens', the subject of a Crusade by the Order of the Teutonic Knights (Christiansen 1980: 169). On the other 'western marches', the Wends had earlier been subject to the first of the new-style campaigns in 1147, promoted by St Bernard formally as 'crusades' and which became a cheaper way of carrying out one's vow and obtaining spiritual pardon than journeying to the Holy Land.

The Lithuanian state expanded to the east, taking over some of the territory of the early Kievan Rus and being joined by some Ruthenian principalities that wished to gain

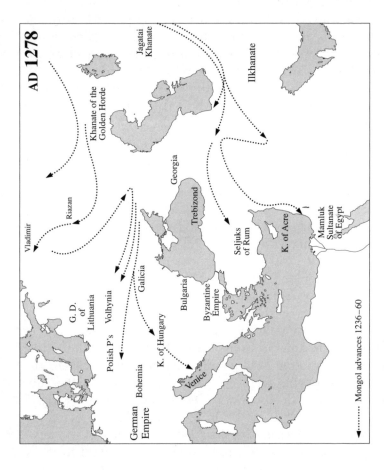

AD 1278

Khanate of the
Golden Horde

Jagatai
Khanate

Ilkhanate

Vladimir

Riazan

Georgia

Trebizond

Seljuks
of Rum

K. of Acre

Mamluk
Sultanate
of Egypt

G. D.
of
Lithuania

Volhynia

Galicia

Bulgaria

Byzantine
Empire

Polish P's

K. of Hungary

German
Empire

Bohemia

Venice

········· Mongol advances 1236–60

1.3 The Mongol Empire

protection against the Mongol Tartars. For it was their victory over the Mongol army at the Battle of Sinye Vody (Blue Water) in 1363 that enabled Lithuania to gain the provinces of Kiev and Podolia, giving them control over most of the Ukraine. The state wanted to take over all the former lands of the Golden Horde, but that aim was brought to an end by defeat at the Battle of Vorsk in 1399. Even so the country extended all the way from the Baltic to the Black Sea, where it held 150 km of the coast.

Lithuania operated in close alliance with Poland, which also played an important role on the international stage when John Sobieski ('the vanquisher of the Turks') defeated the invasion of the Ottoman Turks at the Battle of Chocim in 1673, after a Cossack rising had sided with the enemy; ten years before they had inspired the successful defence of Vienna.

During the period of Tartar dominance, Russian Christian society continued to exist despite the conversion of the Mongol rulers to Islam. Culturally this dominance was thin. There is no evidence that any single Turkish or Islamic text of religious, philosophical, literary or scholarly content was translated into Slavonic or any East Slav vernacular during this period. Politically and economically things were different; in those spheres Christian Slavs and Muslim Tartars engaged in continuing relationships. Contact with Islam even led to a measure of kinship between Christians and Muslims, and the same was true of the sultanate in Turkey, which often preferred to marry out and establish alliances with Christian rulers rather than promote local families to near equality through marriage.

The empire of Genghis collapsed, but Timur, who was another Turkisized Mongol invader, claimed to restore it. But his intervention further north did not last long. He assisted and occupied Moscow, but later fought and took Georgia and surrounding territories. In the end he defeated the Ottoman Turks under Bayezid I (the Bajazet of Racine's play, 1672) near Ankara in 1402, as well as capturing Smyrna from the Knights of Rhodes. The Golden Horde disintegrated by the 1430s, leaving as its three successor states the khanates of Kazan, Astrakhan and the Crimea. This last became a Turkish vassal in 1475. Muscovy still owed them tribute, but this was met in an increasingly perfunctory way. Later, Ivan the Terrible decided it was time to put a final end to Tartar–Mongol rule in central Russia and so occupied Kazan in 1552, establishing his rule over Astrakhan four years later as well as securing control of the waterway to the Caspian Sea. During the sixteenth century Russia set out on an extraordinary and rapid expansion through the forests of Siberia to the north, taking over its hunting and fishing populations, and, aided by Cossacks in their search for fur, reached the Pacific in about 1639, annexing the Kamchatka peninsula by the end of the century and entering the Chinese sphere round the Amur River in the middle of the seventeenth. The whole of Siberia was soon colonized by Russians, although Islamic Central Asia, down to Afghanistan, was not conquered until the nineteenth century and then left largely under its Muslim rulers and culture, despite the Soviet regime's antagonism to religions generally.

During the period of the Russian expansion, the Tartar Confederation continued to be present in what we now understand as Russian Europe. Indeed in the Ukraine, as late as 1664, Peter Doroshenko, a new leader, deliberately put himself under the protection of the Ottomans. The Crimea (which had been allied to Lithuania) also survived until 1783 under the protection of the Ottomans. The Turks joined with them on a number of major military operations, alarming both Poland and Moscow into making a truce. The Tartars continued to form the major part of the Crimea's population even under the USSR until they were forcibly dispersed into Central Asia in 1945 for alleged cooperation with the Germans during the Second World War.

When Peter I became sole ruler in 1694, his first political aim was to secure Muscovy's southern border against the threat of raids by Crimean Tartars supported by the Ottomans. His initial attempt in 1695 failed to establish a foothold on the Sea of Azov because of a lack of sea power.

As a consequence he followed Western European nations in building up a strong navy and so succeeded in capturing Azov a year later. He was convinced he needed to exploit Western technology if he was to defeat the Turks and spent a year in Holland and England to this end. He also extended Russian control along the Caspian Sea at Persia's expense (1723). That expansion was pursued by Catherine the Great (1762–96), who secured the northern shore of the Black Sea, annexed the Crimea (1783) and expanded beyond the Urals. Early in the new century, Russia gained great prestige from her contribution to the defeat of Napoleon. Later she recorded victories in the East against Muslim powers: Persia in 1826, Turkey in 1828–9, the mountaineers of the Caucasus during the 1830s and 1840s. In the first half of the century Russia expanded in the Caucasus: Georgia united voluntarily with Russia in 1801 and Persia ceded northern Azerbaijan, including the Baku peninsula, in 1813 and the Armenian province of Erwan in 1828. The Muslim Chechens, however, resisted Russian expansion for twenty-five years between 1834 and 1859. In the 1840s Russian rule was established over Kazakhstan, which was largely pastoral. In the Far East the Russia-America company explored Alaska searching for fur and even established a Russian fort in north California before that area became part of the USA, giving their name to Russian River.

In this way the Mongol and Turkish advances into Europe were largely reversed, even if Islam remained strong in some pockets. As a result of this reversal, the Muslim countries of Central Asia came under European domination, first of Imperial Russia, then of the Soviet Union, until they finally received their independence with the dissolution of the latter in 1991. In India too, in South-East Asia and in the Near East, Islamic states were taken over by European colonial powers and eventually became free as the result of the weakening of control after the Second World War, the movements for independence and the subsequent process of decolonization. The Near East and Afghanistan remained under the watchful eye of the Western powers, largely because of the nearby reserves of oil on which the developed world had come increasingly to depend, but there too resistance to external domination, especially on the part of non-Muslim powers, came to play a significant part.

Overall the Mongol–Tartar invasion of Eastern Europe in the late Middle Ages led to the dispersion of settlements, to the great emptiness of the region they invested and above all to the weakening of the relative autonomy of kings and great princes (Wallerstein 1974: 977). But there was also a considerable influence on the domestic scene, especially in terms of hygiene and the use of water, about which the Christians had a lot to learn. Writing of the encounter with a trading post of the Swedish Rus in the course of a diplomatic mission to the Khaganate of Bulgar on the Volga, Ibn Fadlan says: 'Never have I seen people of more perfect physique.' But 'They are the filthiest of god's creatures . . . as stray donkeys.'[12] Water, hygiene and cleanliness were more important to the Muslims, partly for religious reasons.[13] The difference between Christianity and Islam in this respect can be seen in Howard's comment that in medieval Venice references to baths and bathing are rare but in Venetian colonies in the eastern Mediterranean they were essential, a difference she remarks that reflects not only climate and water supply but also 'the greater significance of personal hygiene in the eastern religions' (2000: 10).

The three streams of cultural influence

This account has necessarily concentrated upon the physical penetration of Muslims into Europe. We need to look at the cultural influences that accompanied these movements, as well as the influences that came by other means, by merchants, by pilgrims, by embassies and by other travellers. Each thrust of Islam into Europe brought its own socio-cultural implications. The influence of Spanish and Sicilian Islam on Europe is well known. Under the impact of Islam, Hellenistic thought was applied to new questions. The philosopher

Ibn Rushd (*b*. Cordoba, 1126; *d*. Marrakesh, capital of the Almohad dynasty, 1198), known as Averroës, was the *qadi* and physician whose commentary on Aristotle became so important to medieval Europe. In addition there were a number of other significant philosophers writing in Arabic, such as the Jewish Maimonides. The Alhambra palace in Granada was built.

Science and literature were given a boost by the introduction of paper-making that was promoted by the capture of a group of Chinese technicians at the Battle of Talas in Kyrgyzstan in 751. Or the process may have been brought from China by the Mongols to the Near East. In any case, paper was being manufactured in Transoxiana in the eighth century and was being exported from Damascus by about 935, but was not much used in Christian Europe until the fourteenth century.

The manufacture of paper spread west to Sicily in about 1000 and to the region of Valencia in Spain about 1151, when we also hear of water-wheels being used to drive the pulping process (as had already happened in Baghdad about 950); the processes reached England much later, around 1490 (and Italy and France somewhat earlier), and were critical in the expansion of book learning in the Renaissance, especially with the advent of the printing press adapted to the alphabetic script. Paper was much cheaper than other materials and used very widely, for some of the Geniza manuscripts in Cairo, for example. Paper was easy to transport and gave rise to huge libraries. The Fatimid royal library seized by Saladin was said to contain 1.6 million books (Howard 2000: 59). Book production increased and translations into Arabic were encouraged from Greek, Middle Persian and Syriac. Later, with the Christian recapture of Toledo, translations were made by Jewish scholars into Latin. While it is true that the advent of paper encouraged the publication of books, the growth in education (in the nineteenth century Dozy (Eng. trans., 1913) claimed that almost everybody in Cordoba could read and write, but he was mistaken) certainly did the same from the demand side.

Much of scientific importance was transmitted. In the nineteenth century Islam as a religion was thought to be an impediment to economic and indeed other kinds of progress (or rationality), being too conservative and fatalistic. Over the long term that is clearly a very mistaken ethnocentric judgement, in so far as it is applied to the period before industrialization in the late eighteenth century. In any case it implied that every believer's commitment was identical. Mathematical knowledge was developed by Gerbert of Aurillac (*c*.945–1003, later Pope Sylvester II), who had gone to study in Spain. He wrote a book on the abacus which included the use of the numerals we still refer to as Arabic and in particular the use of zero, which was adopted from India (and there possibly from China). Calculation for scientific and practical purposes thus became very much simpler than with the cumbersome Roman system. In the field of mathematics, al-Khwarizmi, from whose name the word 'algorithm' is derived, creatively combined Hellenistic and Sanskritic concepts. The word 'algebra' derives from the title of his major work ('the Book of Integration and Equation'). Arabic gave birth to the words 'alcohol' and 'alchemy', from which the word 'chemistry' comes. Islam had the foremost scholars of medicine, many of whom were Jewish; some were based in Sicily, which set the model for the first Christian medieval schools at Salerno on the Italian coast and possibly at Montpellier on the coast of southern France. Two recent commentators have summarized the scientific achievements of Islam in the following words:

> Muslim scholars calculated the angle of the ecliptic; measured the size of the Earth; calculated the precession of the equinoxes; explained, in the field of optics and physics, such phenomena as refraction of light, gravity, capillary attraction, and twilight; and developed observatories for the empirical study of heavenly bodies. They made advances in the uses of drugs, herbs, and foods for medication; established hospitals with a system of interns and externs; discovered causes of certain diseases and developed correct diagnoses of them; proposed new concepts of hygiene; made use of

anesthetics in surgery with newly innovated surgical tools; and introduced the science of dissection in anatomy. They furthered the scientific breeding of horses and cattle; found new ways of grafting to produce new types of flowers and fruits; introduced new concepts of irrigation, fertilization, and soil cultivation; and improved upon the science of navigation. In the area of chemistry, Muslim scholarship led to the discovery of such substances as potash, alcohol, nitrate of silver, nitric acid, sulfuric acid, and mercury chloride. It also developed to a high degree of perfection the arts of textiles, ceramics and metallurgy. (Nakosteen and Szyliowicz 1997, vol. 18, 16–17)

Already in Charlemagne's lifetime 'the new Arab pharmacology . . . was beginning to make headway with practitioners on both sides of the Alps'; hence the use of the words *azarum* (a resinous gum), ambergris (from Arabic *ambar*) and camphor (Arabic *kāfūr*), the last-named being purchased by Jewish merchants in South-East Asia (McCormick 2001: 714). The first reception of Arab drugs in northern Italy occurred around 800. Evidence from Salerno with its medical school dates from the early tenth century. These imports attest to the importance of the new Adriatic trade route linking Venice to the Muslim world.

Muslim scholarship flourished both in Spain and Sicily. In Spain it was centred on the capital Cordoba, where in the tenth century the culture flourished under al-Hakkam II, second Umayyad Caliph of Spain (961–76), who culled books and scholars from the whole Muslim world. Cordoba became the capital of al-Andalus and its intellectual centre, thanks to the enlightened policy of the Umayyad rulers who encouraged musicians, poets and other scholars. Free schools were provided and learned men brought in to teach at the Great Mosque, which became what has been called Europe's first university college. These developed into the *madrasas*, which had appeared in an embryonic form in the Near East in the eleventh century, becoming widespread in the thirteenth century as schools of higher education, often with hospitals and mental asylums. Vernet writes of one as 'a real university college' (1994: 949). They came later in the Islamic West, but endowments of this kind already existed in Granada by 1349. At that period, the library in the Alcazar, one of seventy in Cordoba, was said to have contained 400,000 volumes at a time when the monastery of St Gall in Switzerland, one of the largest in Europe, had but 600. The discrepancy was enormous (Hillenbrand 1994: 121). Cordoba had paved roads and lamps at street corners some seven hundred years before London had only one, and centuries before it was possible to walk through Paris on a rainy day without getting covered in mud (López-Baralt 1994: 511).

With the fall of the dynasty and the division of the country into small kingdoms, the competition among them grew stronger, and scholarship and the arts flourished. The fall of Toledo in 1085 meant that much of this knowledge passed to Western Europe. Christians who had found themselves under Muslim rule, the Mozarabs, took very quickly to learning Arabic and, much to the dismay of the clergy, Latin was largely forgotten. The reconquest meant that the West acquired its knowledge of Arabic. Many northern scholars then came to study there and the town became a great centre for translating Arabic texts. The first translation of the Qur'an into Latin, a tendentious one, was made by an Englishman, Robert of Kelton, in 1143. Indeed it was the first in any language. It was 'Haly Abbas' who was one of the major channels of transmission of the ideas of Hippocrates and Galen. Meanwhile the Andalusian physician al-Zahrawi ('Albucasis') was noted for his description of surgical instruments; he completed his larger work about 1000 CE and 'revolutionised medicine in Europe' (Howard 2000: 54).

The other great centre was Palermo in Sicily, under Arab domination from 902 to 1071. But the influence continued under the Norman kings. Frederick II corresponded with Arabic scholars in many parts as well as having contacts with scholars from Norman England. That contact led to the court of Henry II and Eleanor of Aquitaine becoming a centre of cosmopolitan culture, with scholars such as Adelard of Bath, who became an enthusiast for *Arabum studia*. He translated Euclid's *Elements* and al-Khwarizmi's astronomical tables from the Arabic.

In a sense the rebirth of learning in Western Europe began long before the Renaissance, and that owed a great deal to Islam and its translations. There was an influx of Aristotle's writings in natural philosophy and science from about 1200, the principal part of which came from Arabic versions and from the commentaries of Avicenna and Averroës. *Metaphysics* and *Natural Philosophy* were banned by various popes, but the ban was never effective and the works served to emancipate the West from the influence of Plato (although only the *Timaeus* was then available). Experience and the experimental method rather than authority were lauded; science was characterized as 'Arabicorum studiorum sensa', 'the views of the Saracens' (Metlitzki 1977: 49).

The transmission of Arab science to Christian Europe was effected by the Latin translators of the twelfth century and was especially strong in astronomy and astrology; the two fields were often scarcely distinguishable, since the latter referred to the study of the influence of the stars on human affairs. Islam developed the astrolabe and introduced Greek knowledge. Copernicus was in turn influenced by the astronomical treatises translated at Toledo under Alfonso the Wise. Catalogues of stars, stemming originally from Ptolemy's *Almagest* (referred to by Chaucer's Wife of Bath), were developed in Baghdad but their onward transmission occurred in the Muslim West, where many English scholars flocked in search of Arab learning (Metlitzki 1977: 77). Such learning was used by Chaucer not only in *The Canterbury Tales*, especially *The Squire's Tale*, set at Sarray in the land of Tartary, where dwelt 'a kyng that werreyed Russye', but also in his treatise on the astrolabe, the origins of which lay in a Latin translation of a work by Mashallah (*d*. 815), an important Jewish astronomer at the Abbasid court in Baghdad. Indeed astronomical treatises spanned the Eurasian world, from Cordoba to Beijing.

Alchemy, as its name implies, was also transmitted through the Muslims. Of the empirical 'worldly' sciences, which ranked below the religious ones, only alchemy, which was the greatest, 'the science of sciences', could be pursued for its own sake (Metlitzki 1977: 90); it held 'the secret of secrets', a guide to spiritual as well as to empirical knowledge. This was the tradition expounded by the Canon's Yeoman in Chaucer's *Canterbury Tales*, bearing witness to the extraordinary impact of Islamic learning on the medieval West in the pre-Renaissance period.

The influence of Arabic medical texts on Europe was also very marked, primarily in Italy and Spain, but from there they spread to the rest of Europe – Germany, France, England and the smaller countries. In Andalusia it was the period between the twelfth and fourteenth centuries that saw the peak of this literary development, in medicine, in dietetics and in agriculture. These texts were of course based on Galen and Hippocrates but did not stop there, as they were adjusted to local products, especially the introduction of rice.

The medical renown of Salerno seems to date from about 870, no doubt due to its proximity to Palermo and the Islamic world, but it was in the second half of the twelfth century that the works of Constantine the African became widely known. Constantine had travelled to Arabia, Persia, India and Ethiopia and ended up in the monastery of Montecassino. He translated a number of works of the Greeks and Arabs, including some by Hippocrates, Galen, ibn Ishaq ibn Abbas and others.[14] He is said to be the first person to transmit Arab medical science to the Western world. In the twelfth century his work passed to Arab Spain and to Europe through the translations of Gerard of Cremona.

In reconquered Spain, the fall of the great centre of learning of Toledo meant that Christian Europe could more easily get access to Islamic technical books, to information about Indian medicine and Hindu numerals, and to Arabic versions of Greek mathematical works and others. Gerard of Cremona lived in Toledo from *c.*1150 to his death in 1187 and organized a team of Jewish interpreters and Latin scribes through whose efforts some ninety books were translated from Arabic into Latin. Islam was always more welcoming to Judaism than Christianity, and under its rule an important Arabo-Jewish culture flourished in both Spain and the Maghrib. But some Arabs stayed on after the reconquest and were employed as translators. Other translations were made in Sicily and elsewhere in Spain. Scholars such as Adelard of Bath used this same store of knowledge for their own purposes, mainly concerning Euclidean geometry and Islamic trigonometry.

The greatest impact of Islam was in agriculture. Here, Europe had a lot to learn. It was Arabs who were experts in water control, irrigation and the associated forms of cultivation. Irrigation was improved and huge water-wheels lifted the contents of canals to the fields. The mechanization of corn-milling spread through the water-mill, thus saving a great deal of labour. The Muslims also brought sugar and its processing to the Mediterranean and developed cotton in Egypt and silk and its weaving in Southern Europe, all processes that originated in India or China. And they were the intermediaries in bringing citrus fruit (e.g., lemons, tangerines, Seville oranges, grapefruit) and other cultigens such as dates and sugar to the region from the East.

Water power too was important in the development of mills and manufacturing before major use was made of other forms of energy. But, above all, water transformed the landscape of Spain, where the development of large-scale irrigation made possible the cultivation of the dry lands into which rice and other monsoon crops were introduced from much further east and needed summer watering. Al-Andalus developed a complex irrigation system and utilized water-mills as well as windmills. But contrary to some writers, the Visigoths before them, and the Romans before that, seem to have practised extensive water control (Lévi-Provençal 1931: 166; Glick 1970), although that was largely for urban rather than for rural ends.

But although the Romans irrigated in Spain, dry-farming was the basis of their agriculture. Roman hydraulic works were directed largely to urban use. But when the Arabs arrived they produced a vast East–West movement of crops which had been grown in India and required water to take them through the dry Mediterranean summers. In addition to the crops mentioned above there were the banana and the watermelon. Hence the importance of irrigation.

There was a great expansion in the use of water-mills in medieval Europe; they are first recorded in the first century BCE, but they only became more widely used first of all in the fourth century, then again after 1000 CE with the widespread adoption of wheat for making bread, the grain of which did not have to be separated by pounding, as did earlier varieties (Parrain 1964). The Muslims actually improved the system and gave their names to most of the local terminology concerning irrigation (such as the water-mill 'noria').[15] Water played a part in the decoration of architectural space through pools and fountains, as well as being used for hygienic purposes. The weaving of silk too spread to Palermo and then to Andalusia. Silk is claimed by some to have been introduced into Spain as early as the eighth century; others suggest the twelfth. From Sicily it spread to Lucca, to Lyons by 1480 and to the rest of Northern Europe.

Agriculture in southern Spain even experienced what was to be called the 'Andalusi agricultural revolution' at the time of the political collapse of the caliphate and the establishment of the petty kingdoms (*taifa*) in the eleventh to thirteenth centuries. The establishment of an Andalusian school of agronomy was marked by the composition of treatises on the subject in the tenth century, obviously based on earlier traditions. At the same time we find the appearance of botanical or experimental gardens which attempted to grow new plants or to improve existing ones, the earliest of which was built near Cordoba by the first Umayyad ruler.

Agriculture in turn was linked to the more advanced sciences, botany, pharmacology (based on Dioscorides) and medicine. Scholars studied the composition of the soil, the use of manures and the processes of irrigation, including the distribution of water which involved devices like the clepsydra or water-clock, which paved the way for the mechanical clock (Vernet 1994: 950).

Claudio Lange has written: 'Western Europe's takeover in
the 11th century is supposedly the result of a number of
ingenious inventions made behind monastery walls, of techniques of work, and of the import of technology originally
exported by the Arabs into the territories they occupied
. . . what remains central here is that, in the 11th century,
Islamic civilization, together with the Byzantine, Chinese
and Indian civilizations, established the First World of the
time, while Western Europe embodied the Third' (quoted
Jayyusi 1994: xviii). In making this contribution the Arabs
and the Turks had long drawn on the settled civilizations
of the Near East before they invaded Europe, which consequently profited from those traditions. For the northern
entry the Tartar-Mongols remained much closer to their
nomadic roots and therefore had less to offer. The Mongol
invasions produced devastating results in Asia, especially in
China, but for Europe there were also some benefits, since
they opened up the Silk Road again in the thirteenth and
fourteenth centuries and as a result communication with
the East became firmly established. That route had been
used in Roman times and was revived in the Middle Ages. It
was possibly as the result of a journey of a papal ambassador
along it that gunpowder and rockets reached Europe, for
we hear of experiments with these in Cologne in 1257, the
year following the ambassador's return. The first European
accounts of powder were written by a friar, Roger Bacon,
but a form of the material had been known in China since
before 900 CE, some recipes appearing in a printed book in
1040. Guns too seem to have been first developed in China
(Pacey 1990: 48) and again to have been transferred with
Mongol rule to Europe (for Islam was at first without these
weapons), but it was the Europeans who appear to have
been the first to have produced cannon, though soon after
these were being manufactured in Turkey.

Some other important inventions may indicate not communication but that parallel developments took place in
Europe and Asia. The European windmill was so different
from the Persian that it could be considered an independent

invention. That may also have been true of the blast furnace and of some aspects of printing, although Needham sees these as being transferred from China (Pacey 1990: 51).

There was an export of ideas back to the East and West, frequently by way of merchants (many of whom were Jewish) – a 'contributing factor in this process was the expansion of Muslim trade' (Vernet 1994: 945). Much of the trade was with the Mediterranean, especially after the rise of the Italian states, principally Venice, Genoa and Pisa, as well as in Marseilles and Barcelona.

Islam played an important role in the so-called expansion of Europe. It had long since explored the Indian Ocean and the China seas. 'Astrolabes as well as compasses, which first appeared in China in the eleventh century, were introduced to facilitate open-sea navigation and map-making. Muslim experience in ship-building for the high seas of the Indian Ocean rather than the quieter Mediterranean was adapted to suit Atlantic conditions' (Birmingham 1993: 16). In these ways Islam contributed to the success of Portugal's leading role in the 'Age of Exploration'. As the first modern European colonizer, Portugal was tied to the Islamic sphere of exchange, which made it largely monetarized so that its bourgeoisie were prepared for extensive commerce.

It has been suggested (e.g., by Briggs 1931, 1933) that Islamic architecture had a significant influence on the development of the Gothic in Europe, with its attachment to the pointed arch, that influence coming either through Spain or through Sicily. In *Stones of Venice* John Ruskin himself first drew attention to the two phases in the Arabic influence on secular Venetian architecture, the first being the period up to the eleventh century when Islam owed much to the Byzantine, a period that was followed by one more distinctly Arabian when 'the shafts become more slender and the arches consistently pointed' (Howard 2000: 2). Howard also emphasizes the many specific features of Islamic architecture that were incorporated into Venetian buildings as the result of its close relations with the East, through traders primarily, but also through pilgrims, travellers and diplomats.

The architecture of the Piazza San Marco, begun in 1225–8, was possibly stimulated by Damascus, with its great Umayyad mosque begun in 706. The use of coloured mosaics on the exterior of the San Marco was another feature.

The Palazzo Ducale has clear allusions to Mamluk architecture in the lozenge tiling and roof cresting as well as to the buildings of the Ilkanid (Mongol) rulers of Persia – for Venetian merchants the Silk Road was very important for trade. Many decorative themes emerged from contact with the East: the use of gold leaf and ultramarine, previously known in Gothic altarpieces, was later applied to merchant houses, following the practice in Damascus and Tabriz; the 'telephone-dial' windows in the façade of Ca Dario (1480s) had been a feature of the Palace of Bashtak (1337–8) in Cairo (Howard 2000: 153). For by the mid-sixteenth century Venice had inherited the Islamic supremacy in glass-making. The Mihrab-type window was adopted in many buildings, while roof space was adapted to the climate in the *altana*.

It was not only public buildings and great houses that were affected. More generally, the residence was turned inward around a patio. Decoration in Southern Europe is much influenced by Muslim abstraction, by its ceramics, by its recurrent shapes. What elsewhere are known as Roman roof tiles are known around Aix-en-Provence by the name of Sarassin. Muslim wall tiles, which were at first decorated with geometric designs, were later adapted by Christians for figurative purposes.

It has been noted that the form of Islamic art lingered on in Spain much longer than in Sicily or in the Balkans or Russia, where they hardly affected the arts of the local populace (except in clothes) even during Muslim domination (Grabar 1994: 588). Many buildings in Christian Spain, however, were touched by Muslim traditions in what has been called Mudejar art, art of Muslim forms within a non-Muslim context. As with the festival play of the Moors and Christians, that style migrated to the New World. What is obvious, as Grabar remarks (p. 589), is that this preservation of Muslim forms took place while Islam itself and those who professed it were being persecuted, often quite brutally, and eventually physically expelled. During this period Gothic from the north appears as an intruder; only with the Italianate taste of the Renaissance were Islamic elements modified.

Dodds (1994b) speaks of Christians living under Muslim rule (Mozarabs) resisting certain aspects of Islamic art, but when Islam had been thrown back, and the situation became more relaxed, they adopted various Muslim forms. Part of this continuation derives from people's aesthetic sensibilities, part from the practical availability of craftsmen trained in the Islamic tradition, as was the case in Norman Palermo.

The influence of Islam did not stop at science, technology, philosophy, agriculture and trade but extended to literature: the translation of Indo-Persian lore promoted the development of *adab*, a name for a sophisticated prose literature as well as for the refined urban manners that characterized its clientele. Moreover, in addition to the translation of scientific texts, the twelfth and thirteenth centuries also saw translations of an Arabic 'wisdom' literature used as exemplars for clerics to supplement their own biblical traditions. These exemplars included fables of animals and birds as well as other tales drawn from an international repertoire; they have been described as 'the first link in a Western chain that leads to Chaucer's narrative art' (Metlitzki 1977: 96). Many of these stories appear to have originated in India and were used in a moral and allegorical fashion in Islam as in Christianity. But they were seen as being part of the wisdom of the East.

Drama and even fiction were not favoured under Islam and little development took place in these spheres, except for that important collection, probably from India, of the *Arabian Nights*, where there is some suggestion that such storytelling had an influence on the European romance. 'That peculiar and arbitrary species of Fiction which we commonly call Romantic', wrote the eighteenth-century commentator Thomas Warton, 'was entirely unknown to the writers of Greece and Rome.' It came instead from 'the Arabians' via

Spain rather than the Crusades (1871: 91), though this idea is disputed by his editor.

Some of these dramas were popular, others literary. In Laroles (Granada), at the fiestas in honour of Saints Sebastian and Anton, there is enacted a version of the struggle between the Moors and Christians which ended with the Moorish king's conversion to Christianity (García 1992). The performance was known throughout Spain and in Palermo; it even spread to the Spanish-speaking Americas (Wachtel 1971). The Turks too were represented in popular drama, not only of the Punch and Judy type but in the festival performances (in the Vivarais, for example) which were taken up by literary playwrights.

Of particular significance on the literary side was Marlowe's *Tamburlaine* (written c.1587, while he was still at Cambridge, and published in 1590). There the Scythian shepherd defeats first Persia and then Bajazet, ruler of the Turkish Empire. Marlowe celebrates the conqueror's ambitions in magnificent blank verse:

> Nature . . . Doth teach us all to have aspiring minds . . .
> Will us to wear ourselves, and never rest
> Until we reach the ripest fruit of all . . .

Bajazet is also the title of one of Racine's great classical dramas, written nearly a hundred years later (1672) and full of 'oriental' intrigue.

The Arab invasion of France was a defining moment for European literature, giving rise to the first known *chanson de geste*, *The Song of Roland*, which tells the story of the King of the Franks's seven-year war in Spain. It recalls how Charlemagne, unable to take Saragossa, was invited by the governor to mount an expedition against the Umayyads of Cordoba. He then negotiated with the Moorish leader, Marsile, for the right to pull back across the Pyrenees once peace terms had been agreed. The story tells how nevertheless the Muslims attacked his rearguard at Roncevalles, where the paladin Roland died defending the king against overwhelming odds. In revenge Charlemagne attacked and reconquered Spain for the Christians. The reality of course was very different. He pulled out of Spain, defeated, sacking the Christian city of Pamplona and attacked by the Basques. The *chanson* is thought to have been composed long after these events, between 1090 and 1130, roughly at the time of the First Crusade, which resulted from the call to arms of Pope Urban II at Clermont. The Crusades formally continued until the eighth was launched in 1263 in an attempt to free the Holy Sepulchre from the Muslims, but as we have seen the notion of a holy war continued long after.

The *chansons de geste*, specifically the epic precursor the *Chanson de Roland*, gave rise to a vast body of narrative prose and verse that accumulated around the legends of Charlemagne and his wars with the Muslims. The same Roland, who famously met his death at Roncevalles, was the protagonist of Ariosto's poem *Orlando furioso* (1532) some four hundred years later. It followed other elaborations of the original legend, such as the *Chanson d'Aspremont* and later works that were influenced by the more fanciful Arthurian tales. Ariosto's poem was a continuation of Boiardo's *Orlando innamorato*, which gives as much attention to love as to war. Ariosto's sequence begins:

> Of loves and ladies, knights and arms, I sing,
> Of courtesies, and many a daring feat;
> And from those ancient days my story bring,
> When Moors from Africa passed in hostile fleet,
> And ravaged France, with Agramant their King.

Tasso did not think much of *Orlando furioso*. Beginning at a young age he composed what he saw as a more suitable epic, *Gerusalemme liberata* (1581), about Duke Godfrey of Bouillon leading his peers and knights,

> That the great sepulcher of Christ did free
> from the arms of 'the Turks and Morians'
> You must from realms and seas the Turks forth drive.

Past Encounters

The 'Turkish threat' was still very much in evidence at the end of the sixteenth century, and Fairfax's translation, as popular in England as the original was in Italy, was dedicated to Queen Elizabeth herself. Tasso's interest in the Crusades had been stimulated by a Turkish attack in 1558 on Sorrento, where he had been born. However, two of his protagonists fell in love with Saracen girls, so the threat was qualified by interpersonal relations.

Saracens are treated seriously in the *chansons de geste* (Metlitzki 1977: 118). Of the ten medieval romances in Middle English of the Carolingian tradition, all involve Saracens, many having Saracen heroes. At this time there were in fact frequent Saracen raids around the coasts of Britain and Ireland, so that it was not only in the romances that the British were acquainted with their activities. In fact the name Saracen was also extended to other types of raider, and we come across 'marchaunz Sarazin' in an Anglo-Norman version. In the eleventh century we even find Arabic inscriptions in the Isle of Man under the Normans. There is documentary evidence of English trade with the Saracens from the middle of the thirteenth century, but even before that Britain was providing the Muslim world with slaves (Metlitzki 1977: 127).

While various tales show the valour and generosity of Saracen warriors, the Middle English romances are 'essentially vehicles of fanatical propaganda in which the moral ideal of chivalry is subservient to the requirements of religion, politics, and ideology' (Metlitzki 1977: 160). They are concerned with 'the triumph of Christianity over Islam'. But the tales from Muslim sources, such as those in the *Arabian Nights*, do not have the same 'ferocious intolerance' as the crusader stories. The same absence of vindictiveness is found in the Byzantine epics. In the West, however, 'the crude caricature of the medieval Saracen flourished in the popular imagination at the very time when the superiority of Arabian learning was taken for granted' (Metlitzki 1977: 166)

Poetry of a lyric genre was equally important. The Arabs had long developed a strong tradition in this area, including

71

love poetry, well before the coming of Islam. Far from twelfth-century Europe having invented love poetry at the time of the troubadours, as has been claimed by many historians such as de Rougemont and George Duby, as well as by many sociologists and psychologists who have pursued the line that part of the uniqueness of Europe lay in its invention of love, or at least of 'romantic love', the genre was well represented in Arabic. In Andalusia there were a number of women poets, most prominently Wallada, a caliph's daughter, who held a literary salon in Cordoba and composed love poetry. Other women too wrote poetry displaying 'a surprising freedom in their expression and fulfillment in their feelings of love' (Viguerra 1994: 709). The Muslim notion of a paradise on earthly terms seems to have been connected with the medieval notion of the land of Cockayne. On the level of prosody it has been argued that 'there are no precursors of troubadour lyric in the west but convincing analogues in theme, imagery, and verse form occur earlier with Hispano-Arab poets' (Nykl 1946).

Especially significant here was the work of the poet and theologian Ibn Hazm (994–1064), who composed love poetry such as *The Ring of the Dove*, which may well have contributed to ideas of chivalric love among the Provençal troubadours. For poets from Spain crossed the Pyrenean border between Islam and Christianity to practise their craft. Moreover, not only did representative figures from the different courts cross the religious divide, but singing-girls, who had a considerable repertoire of songs, were sent as gifts by Muslim rulers to their Christian counterparts. The Provençal court has been described as essentially similar to those that were to be found on both sides in this border region. That fact has a good deal of importance for Europe's mythology of its uniqueness elaborated by generations of scholars, especially from the nineteenth century onwards (Boase 1994).

One abiding legacy of the Arab invasion exists in flamenco music. Much controversy has surrounded its origins. Undoubtedly there is a contribution from north India brought by the Rom (the 'gypsies'). But the use of quarter-tones, on which Stravinsky remarked, is a major feature of Arab music, with which there are many similarities. Another musical borrowing was the *oud*, the Arab lute (from *al-'ud*), which was the first guitar-type instrument to arrive. It was brought both by the Crusaders and through Spain in the thirteenth and fourteenth centuries. One expert in its performance was Ziryab, who left Baghdad, settled in Cordoba and founded the first school for the *oud* and for Arabic singing, as well as introducing the fifth string for the lute. The lute (Old French *laut*) spread into Europe, where it achieved the height of its fame in Italy, France, Germany and England in the sixteenth to seventeenth centuries. It was the Renaissance instrument *par excellence*. Other musical instruments adopted in the West were the oboe, psaltery, cymbals, frame drum, trumpet, hornpipe and nakers; the rebec introduced a new concept of bowing which eventually led to the emergence of the viol family.

The musical influences of the Moors were experienced not only in the folk music of Andalusia such as the *cante hondo* ('deep song'), passionate in character with rhythmic guitar accompaniment, as well as the fandango, sevillana and seguidillas, but also in dances such as the *jota* of Aragon and Navarre, accompanied by castanets. Spanish folk music found its 'classical' expression in the work of Manuel de Falla (1867–1946); it greatly influenced the music of South America and North America, as in Gershwin's *Cuban Overture*.

Metlitzki speaks of 'the intense preoccupation with the Orient as theme, image and metaphor in the romantic literature of the Western world' (1977: 240). In the sixteenth century, European readers were more attracted by books on the Ottoman Empire than anywhere else. Nearly 50 per cent of French travel books of this time had that as their focus (Hamilton 2001: 26). Some indication of the impact of the Turks and Mongols on Western Europe is given by the numerous dramas in which they played a part. Literary influences too went the other way.

The Turks had less direct influence culturally, although their continuing presence in Eastern Europe and the Mediterranean

73

always made them a prominent point of reference for Europe through to the nineteenth century. But because of their situation across Suez, the Bosphorus and further north to the Urals, they became the necessary intermediaries in all exchange between Europe and East, South and South-East Asia. Artistically, the Muslim world had less to teach Europe, partly because of the aversion to figurative representation embedded in Islam. While the Orient formed the subject of European painters from Bellini to Kandinsky and later, Islam did not itself create much figurative art, though it exported some fabulous animals, and later on Mughal painting. However, carpets from the East ('oriental carpets') with their largely abstract designs became great favourites in Europe from an early period, especially so in the Renaissance. So too did jewellery and ceramics. Tartar embroidery was also much prized in the West, and among those items bequeathed by Marco Polo was a white outfit *alla Tartaresca*.

As a result of her contacts with the East, Venice became the great medium for the importation of Eastern art, particularly Byzantine, into Europe, especially in the great basilica of St Mark's, affecting the Renaissance and giving birth to a long line of painters from Cimabue to Giotto. After the capture of Constantinople, Byzantine and Eastern influences became more important for the West. Venice was the only historic port where Turkish merchant ships could dock in time of peace, and the visits were noted by a number of artists. Carpaccio's oriental figures in *The Miracle of the Relics of the Cross* (1494) are taken not from reports but from observations in the streets of Venice.[16] Albrecht Dürer similarly painted *A Turkish Family* from life there in 1511.

Gentile Bellini was the first to introduce the Orient into Venetian painting. In 1479 he accompanied an embassy to Constantinople at the express demand, it is said, of Mehmed II, the Conqueror. He painted a portrait of the ruler in 1580, now in the National Gallery in London, for it was later sold in the bazaar by his son, who properly disapproved of figurative images, and there it was bought by some

74

Venetian merchants. Bellini and others later introduced oriental figures into their works.

European painters displayed an ambivalence about the Orient that represented the wider sentiments, as we have noted. They were attracted to its display, to its costumes, especially in dealing with biblical themes (as in the work of Rembrandt). At the same time there was undoubted fear at the constant threat Turkey posed to the West, at least until the defeat of its navy at Lepanto in 1571 and later on after the breaking of the siege of Vienna in 1683. That fear was a fear not only of conquest but of their reputedly 'cruel' behaviour and cultural influence.

The real beginning of Europe's unambiguous fascination with the Orient occurred at the end of the seventeenth century after that threat had largely disappeared, at least from Western Europe, and after the counter-attack was on its way. The eighteenth century produced a craze for things Turkish (*turquéries*) as well as for things Chinese (*chinoiseries*), both of which became part of the rococo style that characterized the opulence of the *ancien régime*. At this time there was an enormous expansion of trade to the East, from Marseilles and other ports. Ambassadors too wrote accounts of the East; especially influential were the letters of Lady Mary Wortley Montagu from Istanbul. In the same century, but above all in the nineteenth, Orientalism achieved its zenith in painting, especially in attempts to depict Lady Montagu in Istanbul (e.g., by Van Mour) or in the more exotic scenes of harems, baths and toilettes painted by Boucher, Fragonard and, in Italy, the Guardi brothers.

There was also a new vogue for Arabic and Persian literature. In 1704 the first volumes of a French version of *A Thousand and One Nights* appeared. That was the century that also saw the use of the Orient for criticizing the West, as in Montesquieu's satirical *Lettres persanes* (1721). Voltaire likewise employed the appeal of the Orient in his moral tales, *Zaire* (1731) and, most famously, *Candide* (1759). He even wrote an essay entitled *Mahomet*. Diderot followed Montesquieu in using the East to comment on the West.

Past Encounters

In Britain, Dr Johnson chose an Eastern background, though in this case it was Ethiopia, for his moral tale *Rasselas* (1759). In Germany, Goethe used an oriental setting for a volume of poems, the *West-Oestlicher Divan* (1819). Orientalists such as the Austrian, Hammer, spent many years studying in Istanbul during the same period.

Regarding everyday life, the Turkish conquest did have a considerable influence on Eastern Europe, especially on the Balkans, an influence that endures even to this day. According to Rayna Gavrilova:

> The coming of the Ottoman Turks in the fourteenth century, besides its significant economic, political and social consequences, had the undeniable character of a major cultural interaction. An empire, stretching from Persia to Morocco and Budapest, had all the advantages of a common market, including several ecological zones. [The] fifteenth and sixteenth centuries have been an era of intensive exchange, primarily in the everyday culture, including nutrition. Several new crops were introduced – such as the apricot, the melon, rice; new culinary techniques and recipes; new practices – [such] as coffee drinking.[17]

As far as cuisine was concerned, the Turks were heirs to the great tradition of Persian cooking, as indeed were the Arabs. Many aspects of the culture of the Balkan area were influenced by Islam, not only the food but daily life generally. That remains true even today, especially among the continuing Muslim population of Bosnia and especially of Albania (including Kosovo and parts of Macedonia). One of the major changes to European patterns of consumption as a whole brought about by the coming of the Arabs to Spain was the introduction of rice in the tenth century; its cultivation took off especially around Valencia. These changes were incorporated in Andalusian recipe books such as *Kitab al-Agdiya* (García 2002).

In Italy, too, the Muslim presence greatly affected daily life. The Arabs occupied Sicily for two centuries before the

Normans took over in 1091, and even then the Norman emperor, Roger II, wore Arab dress at court, spoke Arabic and cultivated Arabic arts and sciences, employing Arab craftsmen to build the magnificent cathedral and monastery of Monreale (1172). The book of the great Arab geographer Ibn Idris, entitled *The Delight of One who Loves Travelling around the World*, was also known as *King Roger's Book*. Idris discusses the abundance and beauty of Sicily, praising the greatness of Palermo, its buildings and surrounding gardens. It was to Sicily they brought sugar in the eleventh century. It was there that they developed, perhaps invented, spaghetti and *pasta asciutta*, using hard-seeded, gluten-rich durum wheat grown only in Sicily and other hot countries around the Mediterranean. Both macaroni and vermicelli were known as *siciliani*, which in the upper strands of society was eaten with the newly imported forks from Constantinople. On a more particularistic level, Robb (1996: 66–7) reports that Palermo's Vucciria market still produces *panelleria*, fried slices of chick-pea flour, a dish going back to Arab times. Another very significant contribution to European cuisine made by the Arabs was *maccharoni*, a general name given to a variety of pasta, vermicelli, gnocchi, tortelli and others, whose adoption throughout Italy seems to have been the result of transmission by Jewish communities (Toaff 2000: 90ff).

Among other things, the Crusaders brought home oriental ways of cooking, having employed local cooks in the East. Traces of early influence appear in many English foods, in Christmas puddings and mince pies (with their dried fruit from the Mediterranean), marzipan, rice pudding and the mint sauce served with lamb. In the twelfth or thirteenth century a book of Arab dietetics was translated into Latin in Venice by one Jambobinus of Cremona as *Liber de ferailis et condimenti*, originally written by Ibn Jazla, a doctor of Baghdad (*d.* 1100). There were in fact many books on cooking written under the Abbasid rulers of Baghdad, where an elaborate court cuisine was developed by the Arab conquerors largely based on earlier Persian models. That became the aristocratic cuisine of the Arab world.

Coffee drinking was introduced into France by a messenger of the sultan to Louis XIV of France in 1669, who impressed with his taste and refinement. As the result of disappointments arising from the status of this messenger, the king asked Molière to write a comedy ridiculing the Turks and was further disappointed when the dramatist produced *Le Bourgeois Gentilhomme*, which only ridiculed Frenchmen disguised as Turks.

The direct influence of Islam is very clear in the history of food, not only as a source of borrowing but as a source of opposition. Late medieval food, with its addiction to sweet flavours, to sherbets, to golden desserts and dried fruit, was much indebted to the Muslim world. The influence on food is clear from the vocabulary, sherbet from *sharbat*, soda from *suda*; the influence was also there on comfortable domestic furnishing, on cushions, divans, mattresses and sofas. And it was Islam that had brought an abundance of cheap sweetener to Europe, sugar from India to Egypt, Cyprus, Southern Europe, Madeira and then Brazil and the Caribbean. At least for the upper elements in society, recipes had been greatly expanded. Spices too came through Islam from the East. Here too the development of a European *haute cuisine* was in part an opposition to Islamic ways, both by way of a return to classical models and to supposedly European traditions, and on the Protestant side, at least on the part of Puritans, by a rejection of luxury and an insistence on plain living. The Renaissance was a mixture of moral revival and of sensuality, the sensuality of the Graeco-Roman world, bringing back the notion of the male connoisseur of food. In their efforts to revive antiquity, scholars compiled compendia of what their ancestors ate, a source that was satirized by Rabelais when he writes of scholars who had their books brought to the table (*Gargantua*, chapter 23).

In the Middle Ages, Islam was sometimes viewed not as a different religion but as a Christian heresy, various accounts being given of Mohammed's earlier adherence to Christianity, by Langland for example. Contact with the Near East led not only to Islamic science and medicine being incorporated

78

in university studies but also to the extension of teaching about Islamic religion and the languages of the Muslims, principally Arabic. It was at the Council of Vienne in 1312 that an appeal was made for the establishment of chairs in Arabic (as well as Chaldaic and Hebrew) in Europe's foremost universities – Paris, Oxford, Bologna, Salamanca and Avignon (temporally wherever the Roman see happened to reside; Linehan 2001). Almost nothing came of this plan in France, favoured above all by missionaries, until more than two centuries later Postel was appointed professor of Arabic at the Collège Royal in Paris. And in 1599 a chair of Arabic was created at Leiden that led not only to the study of Arabic but also to the printing of books, which was at first forbidden in the Arabic world, so attached were they to calligraphy and to the copying tradition. But Arabic books were printed in Venice using a moveable type as early as the 1520s. The great achievement in Arabic typography was the establishment in Rome in 1584 of the Medici press, which aimed to help the union of Arabic-speaking Christians with Rome and to present some non-religious Arabic texts, while Arabic type was also useful for providing travellers with safe conducts. The printing press was undoubtedly a great boon in this as in other branches of knowledge and education; the initial ban by Islam on its use made it more difficult for Muslims to contribute and to compete with the explosion of knowledge that followed its introduction.

So the East not only constituted a threat to the West, it also held great attractions. These appear above all in literature and later in art. In the literature of the Middle Ages, as we have seen, many oriental tales were incorporated in the sermons that became so important in England in the new millennium, being used as exemplars by travelling priests. Later more historicizing accounts of the East were embodied in the epics and the *chansons de geste* that centred upon the defeat of Charlemagne at Roncevalles in 778. In these works the Muslims were usually presented as brave warriors, as worthy enemies. They might be cruel but they could also be generous.

79

In art and decoration, the East was associated with luxury goods, with colourful carpets, with perfumes, with silks, and later with bright cottons. Oriental carpets played an important part in Renaissance paintings, but they were necessarily the possessions of the rich and powerful. With the large-scale imports of Indian cottons by sea at the beginning of the seventeenth century, the bourgeoisie too began to enjoy the colours of the East; with the Industrial Revolution, colourful cottons, made locally but often using oriental designs, spread through the whole society.

In the Middle Ages 'Christian Europe and the Arab world were in a symbiotic relationship in terms of gold and silver', and it has been claimed that 'in monetary matters . . . the two regions should be treated as a whole' (Wallerstein 1974: 39). We have seen the earlier spread of Arabic coins into Carolingian Europe. Later it was Europe that minted silver, the Arabs gold. Gold came mainly from West Africa, silver from local mines. Both flowed eastwards in exchange for Eastern luxuries for which Europe had few equivalent goods to exchange, apart from raw materials and wool. The sources and quantities of bullion changed dramatically with the European invasions of the Americas; that and the opening of the sea routes led to an increase in the amount of Eastern trade goods coming to the West, especially cotton, porcelain and spices. According to Sarton:

> Many people were alarmed by the inroads the Arabic world had made into the cultural fabric of Europe, and perhaps none more so than Petrarch, though he was seduced in a variety of ways by what he struggled to resist. He lived in a world where the serving of highly aromatic, yellow, sugared food had become imperative, where architecture was now characterized by the pointed arch of the Arabic world, where light poured through jewel-like stained-glass church windows to bathe the worshippers in colour.

The influential work of Wallerstein (1974) on world systems theory divided the modern world into the core (Europe) and periphery (the rest). He sees Europe as creating a capitalist world economy; for according to him capitalism is only possible within that framework, not in that of a 'world empire'. Portugal and Spain were at the forefront of this monetization, even if they did not subsequently lead the industrialization of the continent, which depended on this capital being employed in 'productive' ways rather than for the direct consumption of luxuries. It is a theory that to others has seemed to play down the earlier role of manufacture and trade in Asia, by land but especially by water. That trade, frequently in the hands of Muslims, gave rise to a diaspora of merchants throughout the Eastern seas who were very active in commerce well before the arrival of the Europeans and whose networks certainly involved the use of money and of instruments for long-distance exchange and banking such as were later developed in Italy (Markovits 2000).

In this account I have spoken mainly of the apparent benefits that came from Islam. Obviously there were negative aspects as well. Some would argue that intolerance is involved in all religions, as we can see from the contemporary world as well as from 'the wars of religion' that tarnish our past. That of course is true: the writings of all three major Near Eastern religions contain sentiments and presumptions that today would mostly be unacceptable. We phrase things differently in terms of terrorism and 'ultimate values'. Nevertheless the very fact that these religions centred upon written texts, the holy scriptures, meant that their specialists not only became the custodians of those texts but dominated the whole process of education in reading and writing. In this way they became important figures in the transmission of the entire corpus of written knowledge. It was a long time before knowledge could begin to be released from these shackles, however useful they might have been in the early stages. Secular humanism had been characteristic of the classical civilizations and also made its appearance in Islam at certain periods (Zafrani 1996: 89). Indeed the natural sciences were part of the teaching of the higher Islamic schools as they were in Hindu ones. But a clear division between the secular and the religious, where there frequently continued to be some overlap, emerged only after the Renaissance and the Enlightenment.

There is something more to be said about the contact between peoples of these two faiths. The first is that, although there was hostility, fear and conquest, there were also periods of peaceful interaction. I have discussed the confrontation between the Islamic East and the Christian West which is often seen in terms of conquest, *jihad* and holy war. It was much more; culturally the East had a very marked influence on the West, just as later the roles were reversed. Nevertheless it is often held, especially today, that the value systems are quite different. However, towns in the Near East consisted of multi-faith communities; in Spain, Muslims, Christians and Jews lived side by side over long periods. And where trade and travel took place, the societies interacted with one another, reciprocally and to the advantage of both. In her account of the relations of Venice with the East, Howard stresses that neither side consistently adopted attitudes of superiority towards the other; as trading partners they were equal.

If I have spoken of it in a holistic way, Islam is of course highly differentiated from the theological point of view. The Sunni and Shiite sects differ as much perhaps as Catholics and Protestants, and indeed resembled that division even in some of the details. Just as the Jews did in Europe, the Shiites in Persia and the Lebanon developed miracle plays around the death of Ali, whereas the rest of Islam rejected dramatic performances. Equally, probably under the influence of China, they permitted figurative representations of a visual kind and transmitted this tradition to the miniatures of the court art of Mughal India. As with Christian sects, they fought with one another, treated each other as heretics. Nevertheless, in the face of Judaism or Christianity there was a considerable measure of unity, more so perhaps than in the latter case.

The three movements of Muslims into Europe had very different social and cultural effects. All had great military, political and religious implications. But as far as the wider cultural impact was concerned, the implications were more variable. The consequences of Arab penetration into North Africa, Spain and the Mediterranean were by far the greatest. That was the time when Europe lagged most behind intellectually and economically, and so the arrival of the Arabs was most significant. For the latter were drawing on the results of their advance into West Asia, where they were in touch not only with the civilization of Persia and its ancient roots but also with the inheritance of Greece and Rome on the one hand and to a lesser extent of India and China on the other, the land routes to which they dominated.

The agency of trade

Transmission of knowledge from the Near East to Europe occurred primarily through the Islamic presence. But there was a great deal of contact that involved neither conquest nor yet the other kinds of military struggle we have discussed. The main external point of communication with the East was through Venice, which was dependent on the Eastern trade and maintained a sea route to Constantinople (later Istanbul), to Alexandria (often compared to Venice) and to the Levantine coast over much of this period.

Trade expanded rapidly in Europe, principally in the Mediterranean, after the twelfth century. In the year 1000 there were no large trading towns in Northern Europe. These were situated in the Mediterranean, at Venice, Naples, Spain, Constantinople, Alexandria and Cairo, and along the routes to Baghdad, Basra and the further East. By 1212 they had developed greatly, largely due to trade with the East, and London, Paris, Bruges, Ghent and Novgorod were all important centres in the network. By 1346, North-West Europe saw a great efflorescence of trade as merchants penetrated into Germany and Bohemia looking to purchase metals. By 1485 the French traders of Toulouse, Bordeaux and Ravenna were in the picture, and so too was the Muscovy trade with the Baltic (McEvedy 1992).

Venice was built on trade, and has been described as 'a colossal suq'. She was importing luxury goods from the East as early as the eighth century. In 991 the doge sent ambassadors to 'all the Saracen princes' (Howard 2000: 15). She negotiated a base in Byzantium as early as 1082 and then established a series of trading colonies from Tabriz to Alexandria. She had rivals, especially Genoa, but extended her dominion in the later fourteenth and fifteenth centuries. By the fifteenth century, manufactures began to be exported to the Islamic world – textiles, soap, paper, glass, as well as wood and metal from Northern Europe and olive oil, honey, almonds and raisins from along the trade route. The principal imports were cotton, spices, dyes and aromatics, and salt from Egypt and Syria, as well as silk, slaves and furs from the Tartar region. One sees the way that such transnational cultures developed in the books of Venetian traders, and also in those of pilgrims, which were already in circulation in the thirteenth century (Howard 2000: 17). Using the local language, they treated the problems of travelling *oltremare*, of conducting oneself in foreign ports and especially of getting on with the foreigners. The profit of returning with a valuable cargo, at 35 to 50 per cent on the purchase price of imports, was augmented by the fact that knowledge of the East was itself a valuable commodity.

Venice's commerce was not always approved by the papacy, which regarded it as trading with the infidel. For twenty years up to 1345 there was even a formal ban, but otherwise Venice continued her relationship with the East which had so influenced her way of life, in architecture as in some domestic matters, for the port was known for its seclusion of females (apart of course from prostitutes and working women) – hence the construction of balconies so that they could see something of the world.

Merchants were specially educated for trading, partly as 'apprentices' (learning by experience), partly in schools. The Latin of Venetian merchants may not have been perfect, but they were well educated in accounts. Pacioli's explanation of double-entry book-keeping did not, apparently, refer to a new system but had been practised by earlier generations (Howard 2000: 20). Commerce produced what has been called 'a shared culture of great complexity and richness' (Howard 2000: 21), and that description applied not only to Venice but to the groups with which she traded. In such long-term mercantile relationships, which required more than the dumping of goods or the practice of the 'silent trade' of earlier Africa, both communities flourished and exchanged not only goods but knowledge and techniques. For Venetian merchants the need for Arabic had marginalized the use of Greek and Latin, as we see from the fact that, as in Spanish, many Arabic words were incorporated into the Venetian dialect, mostly belonging to the sphere of trade.

Together with the Cairene Jews, the Arabs also controlled much of the vast Indian Ocean and its trade between Africa, Arabia, India and China before the violent advent of the Portuguese in 1498. They had been at the centre of the South Asian world economy. Islam took control of the north of India at an early date and established trading posts down the west coast, at Malabar and elsewhere. The religion reached the north-west of China too, by way of the Silk Road, but Arab trading communities were also found along the coast of southern China, at Gwangzhou (Canton) and Quanzhou (Zaitun). Muslim traders had none of the prohibitions that inhibited Hindus, for example, from travelling by sea, and in China one of the great voyagers, the seven-jewelled eunuch Zheng He, who reached Africa, was Muslim. The *hajj*, the pilgrimage, placed an obligation to travel on all Muslims and was sometimes combined with trade; more often it opened up opportunities and showed the way. The prophet himself had been a trader, originally working with his wife, a rich widow.

There was an influx of Eastern goods, mainly 'luxuries', perfumes, carpets, and silk and cotton cloth. The last-named became one of the great staples of the sea-borne trade to the East when the route to India by the Cape was opened up after 1497. The larger-scale importation of these brightly coloured materials at the beginning of the seventeenth century changed the domestic scene as well as domestic manners. The use of the fork, much commented on by historians of culture such as Elias and Lévi-Strauss, was probably another of these elements. Flowers too changed the European scene, as we are reminded by the history of the tulip, coming as it did from Turkey. While there were other influences, Islam does seem to have played a part in improving the hygiene of Christians, as well as famously introducing the smallpox vaccine.

East–West relations were also affected by the presence of ambassadors in each other's countries. Venice and Genoa had long held recognized trading ports in the Ottoman realms, as they had done in Byzantium before that. These were supplemented by occasional envoys to the Muslim countries. But early in the sixteenth century, France sought to establish herself in Istanbul on a more permanent basis, and in 1534 an arrangement was made which allowed Francis I to do just this, partly to consolidate an anti-Hapsburg alliance. That embassy henceforth became the focus of scholarly as well as of diplomatic activity. Other great powers followed: England, and then in 1533 the Hapsburg emperor, Charles V, dispatched a diplomat, one of whose successors was Augier Ghislain de Busbecq, from the Netherlands, between 1555 and 1562. The latter collected a great deal of information on Turkey and returned with many manuscripts, including a spectacular botanical codex of Dioscorides, as well as camels, possibly the tulip, but certainly sedge and the lilac. He also studied the language of the Krimgoths and wrote vivid accounts of everyday life. England was followed in 1612 by Holland. The appointment of ambassadors was accompanied not only by diplomatic and scholarly activity but also by the further growth of trade.

Travellers such as pilgrims, and converts such as Leo Africanus (albeit temporary), brought knowledge of the East to Europe. The most notorious of these voyagers was Sir John Mandeville, whose account of his travels raised

many doubts about their authenticity but certainly contained
some useful information, probably culled from other authors.
Marco Polo was another popular author who provided a
detailed account of his activities but on whose reliability
doubts have recently been cast (Hamilton 2001: 35).
Another important element in the transactions between
East and West was the continual flow of pilgrims to the Holy
Land, dating from the first centuries. The pilgrimage, which
resulted in considerable investment in Palestine, eventually
turned into the Crusades. In the fifteenth, Philip the Good
of Brabant, who was fascinated by the Levant and turned his
court into what has been described as 'a seminar for Turkish
studies' (Hamilton 2001: 5), advocated a further crusade
against the Turks. That ideal continued into the sixteenth
century and in 1527 an Antwerp printer published an appeal
to finance such a campaign. The capture of Tunis in 1535
by the Holy Roman Emperor Charles can be seen as part
of this desire to confront the 'infidel'. But meanwhile the
pilgrimage continued and gave birth to an extensive travel
literature. Pilgrims usually started from Venice and later
Antwerp: in the fourteenth century a Venetian entrepreneur
offered to transport and feed would-be 'palmers' for 60
golden ducats; later an Antwerp merchant attempted to
organize a regular passenger service to the Levantine coast.
    Antwerp and the western seaboard received a stimulus
from the opening up of the Atlantic, the rise of Protestantism
and the phenomenon of 'Turco-Calvinism', the belief that
an anti-Catholic alliance might be formed with the Porte.
That aim was simply a continuation of the policy of alliance
that earlier had seen the French king, François I, courting
the Ottoman ruler in an attempt to check the power of
the Hapsburgs. Envoys were exchanged between the Turks
and the Dutch, with the latter proposing a trading centre in
Antwerp to the sultan, whose representatives in turn offered
to support the Protestants against Catholic Spain at a time
when the former were experiencing their iconoclastic riots
in 1567. The Turkish presence in Antwerp was represented
by four Greek merchants, obviously from occupied Europe.

In the fourteenth century the port of Antwerp was already a significant trading centre, along with its more successful neighbours, Ghent, Bruges, and the inland towns of northern France. It rose to greater importance in the sixteenth century. The ruler of the Netherlands, Charles of Austria, had succeeded to the Spanish crown in 1516 and was elected Holy Roman Emperor three years later. His empire now bordered the East, reached to the Mediterranean and included territories in America. Antwerp became 'the commercial metropolis of the world', taking over from Venice, and coming into active contact with the Arab and Turkish worlds. However, these relationships were characterized by 'mixed feelings of dread and attraction'. 'The fear of a powerful religious antagonist advancing ever further north, the prospect of alliances of value, the awareness of the Arab contribution to culture and to science, curiosity about an exotic neighbour, all contributed to the ambivalent fascination of the Levant and North Africa' (Hamilton 2001: 1). It was ambivalence that ran throughout Muslim–Christian relationships.

Values

The East in its various forms continues to be seen as very different from the West in its 'despotic', anti-democratic governments, the absence of freedom and of the Christian concepts of love and charity (*caritas*). Indeed a number of countries have drawn a veil over past contacts with Islam, partly because of the perceived discrepancy in value systems. Here I want to call attention to the many convergences that enabled the different communities to interact peacefully as well as conflictually. The point about charity is simplest to deal with, since it was a duty of Muslims to give to the poor, and many charitable bequests (*waqf*) were established which provided educational, hospital and other social facilities. The notions of love and freedom I shall consider, with particular reference to the studies of Nur Yalman (2001). Regarding the nature of government, it is all too easy to note the arbitrary features of the monarchical and republican regimes of the present Near East, and to ignore the authoritarian regimes of Europe in the not-too-distant past, including the extraordinary efforts of Queen Victoria to install her offspring on the thrones of all the major European powers. Regarding democracy, there is more than one way of consulting the people, in addition to the numerical head counts that are part of the modernizing 'ideology' of the recent West. And it is as well to reckon with the limitations of such methods when we take into account the minority that gave the present president power in the USA, and the way that even the head of the elected government in Britain can threaten a major war without the authority of parliament or the UN Security Council and against the opinion of a majority of the electors. Other systems of consultation would make that impossible. We ourselves prefer frequent elections and changes of government, but we need to recognize the limitations of any system of authority, whether Western or Eastern. Some measure of consultation takes place in virtually all regimes.

It will help to give more substance to this comparison if we turn to the views of Islam on equality, fraternity and freedom, so often seen as markers of the liberal democracies of the West. Writing of equality and love (which in this context is fraternity), Yalman sees these as a 'fundamental aspect of the culture of Islam'. Certainly they are 'translated' into practice in the notion of open access of opportunities for people and of the absence of a group with privileged access to divine truths. That idea has been one of the great appeals of the faith to underprivileged groups such as the Black Muslims in the United States. But that notion does not mean there is no inequality among Islamic peoples. 'In practice, inferiority and superiority are as much a part of daily Islamic experience as any other' (Yalman 2001: 271).

Yalman contrasts these high ideals with the notions of hierarchy and renunciation seen by Dumont (1970) as being fundamental to India, counterpoising the highly idealized

89

formula of Islam on the one hand and that of India on the other. The contrast is between his description of Islam and that of Dumont of hierarchy and renunciation in Hinduism, 'an almost mirror-image comparison of two religious world-views that have intermingled with bitter intimacy for more than a thousand years in the Indian sub-continent' (Yalman 2001: 270). According to Dumont, renunciation, ascetic self-denial, is the religious dimension of hierarchy, allowing for some liberation and permitting 'the specially gifted individual to escape from the strict crucible of caste' (2001: 270). But the reality is less dramatically different. Yalman always recognizes that equality has not been achieved throughout Islamic states, and for India he also quotes a comment on the presence of *bakhti*, through which, despite the hierarchy, those who have fallen from twice-born status might be brought to better condition (Hopkins, quoted Yalman 2001: 277). Equally he refers to the great Hindu traditions of love, of the *gopis* for Krishna, of Mughal miniatures, and he might well have called upon the large body of Sanskritic love poetry (Brough 1968). In other words, contradictory practices and beliefs emerge. However, he does still claim a 'profound contrast in Hindu and Muslim devotionalism', going on to suggest that in the Hindu case it is a minor theme of a great civilization (Yalman 2001: 278).

I want to suggest that we need to modify the stark contrast that Yalman draws between the religious ideologies by taking into account the secular ideologies that accompany them. From the African standpoint, both the Islamic society of Turkey and the Hindu society of India are representative of the post-Bronze Age cultures of Eurasia, which are heavily stratified, however those forms of stratification may be qualified by the religious ideologies. Islam may do something to loosen and even oppose the secular stratification, which for the most part is based on unequal access to valuable resources such as land, always ploughed, sometimes irrigated; there is charity, sometimes revolt, but no effective redistribution. In India the secular hierarchy is to some extent supported by the religious ideology, but not entirely, since it is the literate priesthood who create and carry out the religious rites, as in Islam, and who top the hierarchy. The secular rulers follow. Nevertheless the hierarchy is modified by charity, as in Islam, by the act of giving, as when in a Congress-dominated village in Gujarat, I saw the Harijan, formerly the untouchables, queuing up to obtain the leftovers from the yoghurt-making activities of the 'peasant' Patels. Most significant is the fact that there are two sides to the ideology, *bakhti* and Krishna-worship, both displaying more egalitarian characteristics than the dominant orientation of religion. Then there has always been the outright opposition of others, the long tradition of Indian atheistic thought (see Goody 1998, chapter 11), the long tradition of Dalit (untouchable) opposition to the caste system in which they were at the bottom of the pile.

In other words, the notion of equality, of freedom, was present in Hindu society, even if not embedded in the Brahmin religion, just as the practice and to some extent the ideology of hierarchy exists in Islam. It is these contrary tendencies which are mirrors of each other within each society; the religious ideologies do display contrasts, but if they are considered in a wider frame of dominant religious ideology, plus an alternative, often secular, one, we find both trends present in both societies.

How and why? Because both societies, being dependent upon advanced agriculture and its commercial and artisanal concomitants, are heavily stratified from a socio-economic point of view as well as having political stratification in the form of chiefship, and religious-educational stratification in relation to the written word and to the holy scriptures more generally. But stratification runs up against what are virtually pan-human notions of equality and fraternity among humans (as 'brothers' and 'sisters') which constitute a counter-current in stratified societies, and are based on the idea of distributive justice. From the standpoint of the family, it is linked to relations between siblings ('all men are brothers') rather than between parents (prototypically fathers) and children. One set involves equality, the other inequality, and both are built into social relationships from the family outwards. The imposition of hierarchy by the father is countered by claims to equality on behalf of the brothers. These claims may dominate the lifestyles of a person or a community, or they may constitute a point of ideological reference that does not, however, prevent one continuing to act in a rapacious or consumerist manner. We are well acquainted with these ideological-behavioural contradictions in our own daily lives, as when we decry the pollution that cars make to the environment and jump into our Nissan to go down to the supermarket (which we decry as having taken over the small, personalized shops of yesteryear).

Yalman also elaborates on the concept of freedom in Turkish Islam. The Englishman Sir Adolphus Slade, who served as an officer in the Ottoman navy in the 1820s, wrote: 'Hitherto the Osmanley has enjoyed by custom some of the dearest privileges of free men, for which Christian nations have so long struggled.' He paid a very limited land tax, no tithes, needed no passport, encountered no customs or police: 'from the lowest origins he might aspire without presumption to the rank of pasha.' He compares the freedom, 'this capacity of realising the wildest wishes', to the achievements of the French Revolution and implicitly contrasts it with the West (quoted Yalman 2001: 271).

As Yalman explains, the notion of freedom is connected to that of equality. The 'high ideals of Islam', he notes, 'do turn around the principle that there are no privileged persons in Islam, or rather that a person's worth depends upon the morality of his/her intentions, behaviour, and piety. This may lead to the gates of heaven, but even in the worldly kingdoms, all people, once converted to the belief of Islam – i.e., having "surrendered" (*teslim*) to the will of God – must be given an equal chance to rise in society. Hence the promise of Islam, for instance, to Black Muslims in America and to oppressed peoples elsewhere' (Yalman 2001: 271). There are many other practical significances. You could make a slave a Muslim but you could not make a Muslim a slave. Equally a new convert, as with the Albanian dervishes, could rise to the highest offices in the land, bar that of sultan itself.

One of the most disturbing myths of the West is that the values of our 'Judaeo-Christian' civilization are to be distinguished from the East in general and Islam in particular. But Islam has the same roots as Judaism and Christianity, and many of the same values. If we are thinking of the level of religious ideology, then Yalman points out that not only are equality (and love) and freedom fundamental features of its ethical teaching, but so too is a concern for the individual. About the latter he writes of the Islamic world of the Middle East as being a 'vibe' culture. 'People must relate to each other as individuals', a mode of relating that is seen as *alla Turca* in contrast to that of the West, *alla Franca*, meaning cold, distant, elegant, formal, whereas the 'East is lâübali, annoyingly informal and unnecessarily friendly' (Yalman 2001: 273).

'All the sufis', Yalman writes, 'from the great martyr al-Hallaj onwards, have sung of the sanctity of the individual' (2001: 278). The individual, you may agree, but surely not individualism. The individual is stressed, especially by Sufis, in contrast to the formal teaching of the 'authorities'. However, individualism, in the sense of the headlong pursuit of personal economic aims in a consumer-capitalist context, does not meet with the approval of Islamic scholars, whose antipathy to the West may be based on this difference of aims. I do not suggest that there is no conflict here with the aims of the masses to improve their conditions, as they would see it, just as Christian theology concerning riches differs from the aims of the majority of the followers of that religion. But one ideological element within Islam stresses the puritanical values of restraint and simplicity. When he returned to Iran, the Ayatollah Khomeni made a great impression by leading a very humble existence, and is said to have dined on a simple meal of bread and yoghurt in the evenings. Yalman reports even a large and rapacious landlord as saying, 'I am an old man. My needs are few. All I need is a piece of bread and a bit of cheese to keep me going'

(2001: 274). The values of puritanism, of charity, of love and freedom are present in Islam as they are in Christianity. Neither faith has the monopoly of positive aims, nor yet of more negative ones.

I have tried to outline some of the effects, intellectual and technical as well as political, that Islam has had on Europe over the centuries. It cannot, as the late Pim Fortuyn of the Netherlands would have us believe, be considered a 'backward civilization', except in the sense that all civilizations could be thought to display some backward aspects. It is argued by some that religion is a chimera in world affairs; that the real reason for a *jihad* is economic or perhaps political. Such aspects were, of course, always present, but it is impossible to reduce events to those dimensions and to dismiss the ideological factor which has motivated so many, so explicitly, so consistently, so firmly, not only in the religious but also in the political domain.

These three movements of Muslims from the Near East to Europe can be considered as being continuations of earlier tribal movements from Asia to Europe of the kind discussed in McNeil's *Europe's Steppe Frontier*, a 'frontier' that was open to continual penetration from the drier regions of Central Asia. So to some extent they are. But those earlier movements eventually led to their participants being incorporated in Europe in quite a different way. They did not have the ideological commitment of a written world religion. From this point of view the coming of Islam into Europe is better compared to that of Judaism and Christianity, which did not lead to incorporation into earlier regimes but rather to conflict, opposition and conversion. So the movement had a different dynamic which cannot be explained away by so-called ethnic factors; the religious had a significance *sui generis*, an ideological importance which contemporary secularists may not always appreciate but which nevertheless exists for the actors. Just because of our own disbelief or scepticism, religion has to be taken very seriously as an element in the constitution of the country, of Europe, of the world in which we live. Islam was never simply the Other, the Orient, but an element of Europeans, not only part of our past but of our present too, in the Mediterranean, in the Balkans, in Cyprus, in Russia. We need to appreciate its significance and accept the relationship, even if its influence has had a strong religious component to which we may be antipathetic.

Migration in Europe today

The penetration of Islam into Europe had been largely repulsed in earlier times, with the reconquest in Spain and in the Mediterranean, with the demise of the Turkish Empire, 'the sick man of Europe', and with the withdrawal of the Mongols to Central Asia. There has been a small but continual flow of Muslims into Western European countries as migrants, setting aside captives, sailors, merchants and ambassadors. This flow increased with the expansion of colonial rule over Muslim areas. It was a Muslim, Dean Mahomed (1759–1851), who started the first Indian café in London. Well before that there had been a Lascar element in East London, probably as early as the 1600s, when the term became used for East Indian sailors. There was also a small professional immigration from the British Empire. The first attorney in Britain to swear on the Qur'an did so on his admission in 1850. The first mosque was built in Woking in 1895, funded in part by the Emir of Afghanistan.

Some immigration continued from colonial territories, but the massive increase in the recent influx of Muslim immigrants into Europe began in Britain after the Second World War, after their home countries had become independent. The influx then is a feature of decolonization, of post-colonialism. Later it extended to Europe, primarily to Western Europe. Now the European Union is contemplating including Turkey, as well as states like Cyprus and Albania with large Muslim populations. However, in recent years Islam has already made a striking come-back through the immigrants that have moved into a Europe increasingly unable to maintain its workforce. Some superficial index of this penetration is given by the impact of Near Eastern food. Today such restaurants proliferate in our cities, Cypriot, Greek, Turkish and Lebanese, now North African and Iranian, brought by numerous migrants coming either as political or as economic refugees. In France this growth has been described as 'the conquest of France by couscous'. Especially important has been the cooking of skewered meats, kebabs, over charcoal, said to have been invented by the Turks as a food for the battlefield. But from the fourteenth century the Turks also developed a court cuisine, based on the Persian of the Sassanid dynasty as early as the seventh century, and much later there emerged a restaurant culture which subsequently took root in Western Europe.

This immigration has seen national policies vary between the pluralist and the assimilationist. The pluralist nations have not insisted upon integration in the same way as the assimilationist, and allowed for multi-culturalism. The former are represented by the Dutch and the Germans, the latter by the French, who with their republican tradition insist that the state requires the full participation of each citizen in its basic secular traditions; so that it is in France that the wearing of headscarves in schools has given rise to most conflict, whereas in the Netherlands it has largely been ignored or held to be an aspect of religious freedom. In pragmatic Britain headscarves have sometimes been allowed if they display the school's colours (Rath et al. 2001: 4).

Despite these different policies of the host countries, similar questions have been raised throughout the region. These questions relate to places of worship (and in some parts to their financing), to schools and the language of religious instruction (it is Arabic for the Qur'an), to the slaughter of meat (*halal*), to the circumcision of males and to the Muslim festivals, as well as to the application of Muslim law more generally. Whether assimilationist or not, each society is forced by its immigrant population to adjust to these problems, partly because the very nature of the immigrant situation has in many cases led them to place increasing emphasis on their Islamic beliefs and relationships. International links with Islamic states have helped conserve and extend Muslim institutions; the immigrants too have become more conscious of their Islamic identities in a local situation which may claim to be secular but which celebrates Christian festivals on a weekly and annual basis, as well as allowing schools and lessons which tend to promote a version of Christianity. There was initially a 'fiction of temporality' under which both hosts and migrants thought of the latter as returning to their home country, so they usually maintained relationships with this in view. When temporary became permanent, so too their involvement with the new societies changed. Those relations became more politicized with the publication of *The Satanic Verses* by Salman Rushdie and the subsequent *fatwa*, by the bombing of Tripoli by the Americans, and of course by the running sore of Palestine. Politicization did not await the coming of Bin Laden, and that politicization inevitably had its radical side. Let us see how matters developed in specific countries.

Into France have come some six million immigrants, overwhelmingly from its former colonies and dependencies in North and West Africa; Germany has conditionally welcomed two million 'guest workers' from Turkey; Britain has accepted approximately the same number of Muslims from the Indian sub-continent, also formerly a dependent territory. There are problems with these figures, which vary with different sources and apply at best to the numbers originating in Muslim countries. But in fact many became practising Muslims as immigrants, since Islam and attendance at the mosque were aspects of their new identity.[18] In France that is part of the 'sedentarization' of Muslims that followed restrictive measures taken as the result of the petrol crisis of 1973, which meant that many North Africans no longer regarded themselves as temporary residents but wanted a more permanent place in the host country.

All of the new Muslims come as suppliants for work and living space, often taking up positions in the host society which its own members no longer wish to fill. The religious map of the continent has changed radically. Mosques have become a feature of the main towns; so too have Islamic schools and centres, as the Muslims attempt to conserve their religious identity in a context of predominantly Christian expectations. Schools may begin with a 'non-denominational' service, but it is nevertheless Christian in its broad content. The festivities observed throughout the land are based upon the Christian scriptures; Christmas, Easter, All Saints and lesser ceremonies, together with the Christian week, determine the rhythm of work and leisure activities. In such a world Muslims have to fight to maintain their identity and their faith.

It would be impossible even to outline the present situation of Islam throughout the continent, but as examples of what is happening I take two countries – one, France, where the impact has been stronger than in others, the other less so, namely Italy. In France, as in most of Europe, Muslims are very divided and attend different mosques, partly according to nationality (or ethnic group), partly according to 'sect'. Of these the major divisions are between orthodox Sunni and Shiite, the followers of Ali, son-in-law of the prophet. A similar range of Islamic groups seems to emerge in Europe as appeared in Afghanistan, where, following the takeover by an 'independent' Marxist government in Kabul in 1978, six main parties emerged, two led by Sufis, two by clerics, two by students (Edwards 2003). That range is also found in France, but one of the other most important divisions there is the Salafist, who are ultra-orthodox and include the puritanical Wahhabis (founded 1744), supported by Saudi Arabia, and seen as including radical activists; the sect, which is organized in small groups, has been growing recently in France and appeals particularly to the young.

Opposed to the Salafists is the Muslim Brotherhood, founded in Egypt in 1928 and devoted to the modernization of the Sunni sect, but nevertheless with fundamentalist tendencies. They again are opposed by the various Sufi brotherhoods (Sufi, 'weavers of wool') going back to the eighth century and offering a mystical, quietist, version of Islam. One group of Sufis is known as the Habach, originating in Lebanon in the 1970s and strongly supported by Syria. They have been very active against other groups in France, especially the Salafists, and have also tried to convert the young. A fourth sect is that of the Tabligh, a preaching movement originating in India in the 1920s.

Between most of these groups there has been considerable hostility and violence, the Sufis regarding the Wahhabis as 'heretics', the Sunnis considering the Shiites as the same; most contain radical elements, Islamists or fundamentalists, who have acted against non-Muslims, Jews in particular. But the majority of Muslims in France do not belong to any group, nor do they attend a mosque; they are for a measure of integration into the republic.[19]

Some of this differentiation has centred on places of worship. The most important is the Great Mosque of Paris, founded in the 1920s, when France already viewed herself as a 'Muslim power' as a result of its interests in North Africa and the Near East. After some confusion about its management, the Algerian government (from whence the bulk of Muslim immigrants came) took over in 1982. Attached to that central mosque were many other places of worship. Another important association was the Islam Cultural Association of Belleville, which managed the mosque Stalingrad (it is in a communist quarter) and the group Faith and Practice, which in turn was affiliated to the world-wide movement Jama'at al-Tabligh, the Society for the Propagation of Islam, a pietist movement originating in India.

Already in 1987 there were more than 1000 mosques and places of worship in France. More than 600 Islamic associations were registered with the prefecture and in Paris a muezzin called the faithful to prayer five times a day on the local radio. There has been a spectacular increase from the early 1970s; since that time mosques have even appeared in factories such as Renault at Billancourt, itself formerly a shrine to the communist working class. That development has again been attributed to the recognition by immigrants from Islamic countries that they had now become permanently settled in France (Kepel 1991: 11).

The French government has recently made strenuous efforts to organize a central Muslim council that would provide a unified point of communication between all these different elements and the state, in the same way as was earlier done for Catholics, Jews and Protestants. An arrangement was reached in December 2002 to create 'Le Conseil Français du Culte Musulman', presided over by the rector of the Paris mosque, supported by Algeria, with two vice-presidents from the UOIF (Union des Organisations Islamiques de France, supported by the Muslim Brotherhood) and the FNMF (Fédération Nationale des Musulmans de France, supported by Morocco), the two other main associations in the country. The general secretariat will be organized by the Comité de Coordination des Musulmans Turcs de France. The Association of African Muslims will be responsible for international relations, the leader of the Lyons mosque is treasurer. There are representatives from all the five major mosques and seventeen posts for various federations. Only some young Muslim groups have stood aside.

The main problem discussed in relation to these immigrants, once they have arrived, is integration. Have they become French, Dutch, English or German? It is often difficult to know what is meant by this question. Some have not learnt the local language, but that is clearly a transitory phenomenon. Some immigrants from Pakistan support that cricket team rather than England. That too is a transitory matter; it is not long before they are actually playing for their new country. Muslim religion is a mark of difference and doubtless many will continue to hold to that faith, like Jews. But, like Jews and Christians, others will become secular non-believers or non-attenders. However, religion is bound to remain a focus of differentiation, with its adherents attending the mosque (rapidly increasing in number) rather than the church, with many women continuing to cover their hair, and both sexes demanding ritually pure (*kosher* or *halal*) meat. Similar practices have long been tolerated by

Past Encounters

other religious communities, by Jews, by Sikhs and others. But with a total of 10 per cent Muslims in the French population, one needs also to ask how the host society will integrate with its immigrants. As we have seen, efforts have been made to establish a general council for Muslims, thus adapting the political system. But will the whole range of 'national', that is Christian, festivities have to be modified to include the celebrations of other faiths? Already this practice has been adopted in some schools. Will it eventually change the practices of the whole community? It is difficult to see that 'multi-culturalism' will not move some way in this direction, a direction that would certainly do much to make Muslims (and other minorities) feel at home and less alienated.

The problem posed by contemporary Islamic immigration to Western Europe is seen most explicitly in France, and in particular in 'the crisis of the headscarves'. Should the state insist on assimilation, that is, forbid the wearing of discriminating clothing, especially that which indicates religion, or should it adopt a more multi-cultural approach. The traditional republican line demanded secular conformity, but others on the left did not insist on expulsion from schools for wearing scarves. The tone of the debate was highlighted by the fact that, for many, the 'veil' (in fact, the headscarf) was seen as a sign of the inferior position of women under Islam and therefore doubly defying the spirit of the constitution. But while a majority of the French public were against the practice, the Jospin socialist government and the Council of the State made various compromises, although these measures did little to appease the more radical Muslims.

In fact there has already been a great deal of assimilation, much of it through the schools for the second generation. But the schools themselves are also a source of difficulty. It is there, above all, that one's identity is established *vis-à-vis* other groups. It is there that the wearing of the headscarf marks a girl out from her classmates. Many French are devoted to the particular tradition of 'laicism', of separation of church and state; in fact that was only nationally proclaimed,

101

after the revolution itself, in 1905. However, republicanism has always stressed this separation, with the state trying to offer similar opportunities for citizens of all faiths. The role of the Catholic Church has continued to be important for many citizens, even in some secular matters, but nevertheless the wearing of the Islamic headscarf has been seen as a threat to the unity of the republic, just as was the recognition of ethnicity in the 1970s (and, for Chevènement, any concessions to Corsican demands for autonomy). Consequently the 'war of the headscarves' was not only a question of the integration of Muslims, who had to behave publicly as French, but also of the nature of the republic itself. The struggle opened in earnest when the headmaster of a college at Creil in northern France sent three young girls home for wearing them. An attempt was later made by the head to arrange some compromise, but many sympathetic organizations came to throw in their weight and the affair became highly complex, raising consciousness on both sides.

Apart from this history of the 'war of the veil', the more general problem of assimilation as against co-existence, which is virtually irresolvable in respect of members of another religion whose beliefs touch upon matters of life and death as well as of heritage and identity, cannot easily be compromised in Europe other than by people's becoming agnostically 'Christian'. In France the impact of Islam has had a more direct influence on national affairs than in Britain. The communist stronghold of the Renault manufacturing works at Billancourt recruited large numbers of Muslim immigrants, as a result of which mosques and prayer-rooms have been installed in the factory. The strikes of 1982 were attributed by some to this 'subversion intégriste'. Indeed the fact that the subsequent victory of the unions was celebrated with a communal prayer demonstrates that the actors themselves saw Islam as a potent force in their labour dispute. Certainly immigrants were no longer seen as a docile workforce by employers but demanded their rights like anyone else; part of their confidence came from Islam, perhaps from a rebirth of Islam in the migrant context.

While other European countries such as Germany have different models of citizenship, the problems arising from the expression of religion are still present, partly because Muslim law allows practices such as polygyny which laws deriving from the Christian church have prohibited (Goody 1983). In any case those different practices are changing under European pressures. In the eighteenth century, Germany had already recruited a number of Turkish soldiers captured in the various campaigns as well as Mongols from Poland (Sen 2002: 11). In the later nineteenth century the Orient-Politik of the Kaiser led to a heightened rhythm of contact with the Near East. And after the First World War, in 1922, the Islamische Gemeinde Berlin was founded, mainly by students and traders. Berlin was also the location of the first mosque; today there are some 2200 places of worship. With the award of citizenship to Turks living in Germany from 2000, Islam has become eligible for state finance along the same lines as that specified in the agreement between Catholics and Protestants worked out at the compromise of Augsburg (1548) and embodied in the present post-war constitution. Islam then will become a rich and powerful institution.

I have suggested that one of the interesting features about Islam in Europe is that the immigrant situation has itself often led to a greater Islamization, by no means always fundamentalist but including some radical elements. The 'demand for Islam' both in Germany and in France has been seen as a compensation for the earlier exclusion of Turks from citizenship in the first case and for the need to renounce Muslim law and accept the Code Civil if an immigrant took on French nationality (Leveau and Mohsen-Finan 2001: 12). That aspect is certainly present in the rebirth of Islam in Europe but it must not be taken too negatively. There are also positive features about Islam and their own traditions of which the immigrant situation makes people aware. There is pride as well as the reaction to perceived rejection.

Tietze, for example, shows how, for the unemployed, excluded youth, the hours of prayer and the attendance at the place of worship gives meaning, in time and space, to an otherwise unstructured life in the deprived suburbs (Tietze 2001). In Germany, the Turks approximate more closely to their local counterparts, but they do suffer from discrimination which leads them to seek the same comfort in Islam as those in France.

Consciousness of being Muslim in Europe was greatly raised by the Iranian uprising against the Shah of Persia which brought in a puritanical regime devoted to the Sharia, the religious law. Known as 'le mouvement iranien', this change of regime showed the dynamism of a polity based on the Qur'an and gave comfort to those who saw the Muslim East as offering some counterbalance to the dominant, globalizing, Christian West. 'On the part of Muslims', wrote Kepel (1991: 18), 'the Iranian revolution gave birth to considerable enthusiasm, gave pride in their religious faith to a number of people who otherwise would be ashamed of the devalued view of Islam they were faced with in the West.' That was a time when petro-dollars from Arab countries helped to support Islamic associations and when Islamic awareness grew rapidly; 1989 has even been described as 'a Muslim year' (Kaltanbach and Tribalat 2002: 188). In schools, it was 'la guerre du foulard', the war, or the crisis, of the headscarf. Somewhat tendentiously, Kaltanbach and Tribalat use the term veil (as in the title to chapter 6, 'Le voile et la république'), but it was never that. However, certain schools regarded the wearing of the headscarf as a threat to the exclusion of religion from schools, as demanded by the republic. The wearing of a headscarf suddenly grew more popular, in Turkey, in Algeria, in Britain, throughout Europe. Many saw this as a threat not only to a 'humanistic' education, but to internal peace. Not only did it represent a refusal to 'integrate', to do as others do, but possibly indicated an attachment to 'terrorist' causes and certainly a raising of consciousness. This was the year that saw a conference of European Muslims in the Netherlands, the aim of which was to try and get themselves recognized as a community with a legal status. Gradually that change is taking place.

Past Encounters

We are accustomed to think of Islamicist ideas as being spread by a handful of bearded clerics in the mosques of the larger cities. But, like the rest of the world, radical Islam has gone electronic and broadcasts its ideas via the internet, available in every cyber-café in town or every computer in the home. Kaltanbach and Tribalat devote a special chapter to 'L'Islam des internautes', listing some of the various websites propagating Islam, especially the Centre Islamique de Genève, which appeals to an international audience, bringing together fighters from Bosnia, Chechnya and elsewhere. Khosrokhavar, too, in his account of *Les Nouveaux Martyrs d'Allah* (2002), stresses the role of the internet in making radical Islamic ideas available to the diaspora, a medium that, because of its addiction to the 'virtual', increases the degree of radicalization of its message (2002: 324, on the 'néo-umma transnationale') since it tends to decontextualize ideas and to confuse the boundary between game ('starwars') and reality.

The recent advent of Muslims in Italy has been chronicled by Allievi and Dassetto in *Il ritorno dell' Islam: i musulmani in Italia* (1993). It is a return because Islam had been estab-lished in Sicily as early as the first visit of 'Saracens' in 652 CE. The capital Palermo was known as 'the town of three hundred mosques' by Ibn Hawkul, an Arab traveller in the Norman period. Conquest was followed by 156 years of domination, but the influence of Islam continued well into the Norman period, being especially important in the reign of Frederick II.

Islam spread to the mainland as well with the Emirate of Bari and to the far north in the Valley of Aosta, where small groups of Muslims had come from France. There is even mention of mosques up until the eighteenth century, espec-ially 'the mosques for slaves' in coastal towns such as Genoa, Livorno and Naples.

Of course, Italy was always geographically close to the world of Islam, and the city of Venice conducted continuous commerce with the Turkish capital of Istanbul (and with Constantinople before that) as well as with other ports on the southern shores of the Mediterranean. But in the modern period Italy made little obvious effort to establish colonies in that area, though she did occupy Eritrea in 1885 and Somaliland from 1889, invading Ethiopia in 1895. Italy invaded Libya, still under Ottoman domination, in 1911. That was followed by Mussolini's grander imperial ambitions and the desire to make the country 'a great Islamic power' and the Mediterranean into 'our sea'. Unlike the case of those other imperial powers Britain and France, these adventures did not lead to a great influx of Islamic refugees in the period after the Second World War. However, since then there have been some immigrants from Albania and others from Somalia, both of which constituted part of the scene of Italy's conquests overseas, but the majority of Muslims have come from Morocco, Tunisia and the former Yugoslavia, perhaps 96,000 in the first case and 50,000 and 45,000 in the other two. The migration has been rapid, as we see from the growth in the number of mosques and places of prayer in recent years. Before 1970 there was only one (at Rome); by 1994 there were some sixty mosques and 100 to 120 places of prayer, often associated with particular national groups. The growth of mosques served some quarter of a million faithful and has been stimulated by the Unione degli Studenti Musulmani in Italia (USMI), founded in 1971 and located primarily in university towns, and receiving funds from Saudi Arabia and Libya, as in many other cases elsewhere.

The Muslims in Italy constitute the second most numerous religion in the country and belong to the same wide range of sects, movements and fraternities (*tariqa*) as in France. Numerically the most important of the *tariqa* is the Tijanniyya, but also of great significance among immigrants from the Senegal are the Murides, who are heavily involved in organizing their members for petty trading activities, here as in other parts of the world. The Murides collect contributions from their employed members which are paid to the local sheikh. He organizes a range of welfare activities for the members, who draw benefits from this 'friendly society'.[20] Other groups too may be linked to a charismatic leader or to the imam of a mosque.

Past Encounters

The Murides (from *murid*, seeker after God) are of special interest, since they spread throughout Europe as well as to New York and Hong Kong. They belong to a Sufi brotherhood from Senegal, from whence the earlier Almoravids came to conquer Spain. These itinerant traders are organized around a founding saint, Sheikh Amadu Bamba (*c.*1857–1927), whose followers were initially very successful in peanut farming in the early colonial period. The conditions of production and trade grew worse, and many abandoned agriculture and now belong to an international trading diaspora. They succeeded because of hard work, discipline and prayer, as well as through their efficient organization. The members (*taalibe*, disciples) are organized into 'circles' (*da'ira*) around a particular sheikh whom they support and with whom they keep in contact. The sheikhs generally visit their scattered circles once a year (O'Brien 1971).

The majority of the Murides are street peddlers but some have reached higher ranks in business. They deal in items that are small in size and produce a quick turnover, such as Asian watches and novelty items. Some Murides have become students, some work in other jobs, most still support themselves by trade (Ebin 1996). They return to Senegal from time to time to visit their holy city of Touba. While abroad they limit their contacts with the outside world and keep mainly to themselves.

Various movements, some of which are more political, others more religious, have spread throughout Italy, in particular the Jama'at al-Tabligh and the Muslim Brotherhood, as well as militant groups within the student organization who distribute Islamic literature. There are other movements connected with organizations such as Hamas and formerly the Afghan *jihad*. On quite a different level of sects we find groups of Shiites, but very few that relate to the countries of origin, unlike the situation in other European countries. At a yet more inclusive level of association there is the high status, 'diplomatic', Centro Islamico Culturale d'Italia, which has existed since 1966 and is in the hands of Saudi Arabia, as in most European capitals. This conservative body is opposed by a new one, Unione delle Communità e delle Organizzazioni Islamiche in Italia (UCOII), founded in 1977 but including older groups (among whom are the students). This radical group opposes the Centro as consisting of representatives of Islamic politics, of ambassadors, of persons compromised with Europe and the enemies of true Islam. It is this organization that is most prominent in the media.

The fact that in Italy as elsewhere groups of Muslims receive support from other Islamic powers – France from Algeria, Saudi Arabia and Syria – could be taken as interference by those nations in the internal affairs of the host country. But we have to put this aid in the context of the contributions of Jewish communities to Israel, long seen as interference by Palestinians and by other Muslim communities, as well as the aid offered by Western countries to missionary groups scattered throughout the world (and seen as a particular threat in China, India and some Arab countries).

Such external links are inevitable within written world religions whose boundaries necessarily stretch beyond those of nations or of ethnic groups and, as we have seen, are often of an enduring kind. That is even true of Hinduism, despite the absence of any overall religious organization; not only are immigrants, to Britain for example, drawn back on pilgrimage to various Hindu shrines (where these cannot be replicated locally) but wealth too returns in quantities large enough to make a substantial contribution to the country's balance of payments. Such a plurality of allegiances has to be accepted in the modern world, since they exist and would be difficult to eliminate, especially in view of the respect for cultural difference (multi-culturalism) which has become part of our more globalized network of communication and social space, our eating habits and our travel for business or for leisure.

Today Islam in Europe is an important religion with many adherents. Those followers range from the conservative to the radical, the latter being strongly opposed to the treatment of the Palestinians in the Near East and always providing a potential recruiting ground for violent and militant action, of the kind discussed in chapter 3. Their situation requires some kind of formal recognition on the part of the state, at least on the same level as that of the Jewish communities. While such recognition will not lead to the abandonment of Muslim causes throughout the world, it might help to lead to political rather than to violent action in their support. In any case we need to recognize Islam as part of our present as it has been such a significant part of our past. That process will involve some difficult adjustments which follow from the need for an overseas labour force drawn largely from former colonies or 'territories of influence', as well, of course, as from more generous inputs leading to the provision of a refuge for those in need.

More recently, Islamic activism has taken on a pan-European direction with the founding in 2001 of the Arab European League by Abou Jahjah, a Lebanese immigrant with a degree in political science and Belgian nationality. His aims, he declares, are neither extremist (fundamentalist) nor integrationist. Like his model, Malcolm X in the United States, he is against integration but in favour of Islamic pride. The demands include Islamic schools, bilingual education for Arab children, hiring quotas for immigrants and the recognition of Arabic as an official language (German is already so recognized on the basis of a much smaller minority). So far the movement too is relatively small, with no regular headquarters but meeting, significantly, in an Antwerp internet café (*International Herald Tribune*, 5 March 2003). Small as it is, it represents a new activism arising out of the immigrant situation which events in the Near East will only help to stimulate.

2

Bitter Icons and
Ethnic Cleansing[1]

Icons

It was a recent visit to Cyprus, to the ancient monastery of
Chrysoroyiatissa, in the hills above Paphos, that led me to
think about the role of Islamic iconoclasm, of the objections
if not to the images themselves, at least to their worship, in
the conflicts between Christian Greeks and Muslim Turks in
Cyprus and to the splitting of that island, some hope in a
temporary way, between the two communities as a result
of a drastic process of 'ethnic cleansing'. And what is the
'ethnicity' here that keeps people apart?

In the reconstructed church of the monastery, which
had been damaged by earthquakes as well as by the bombs
of what are referred to as the Turkish 'hordes' in 1974
when the island was split, the icons, figurative representations of saints and the sacred, decorated the iconostasis
dividing the congregation from the Lord's table. Many local
pilgrim-tourists came in and bent their heads over first
the main icon near the entrance, bestowed a holy kiss upon
it and then did the same to a selection of the other icons
on the main stand. Here was not only the acceptance of
figurative representations but also their worship or reverence in a human manner, as if they were living beings, or

110

were the represented beings themselves, rather than a simulacrum, an effigy.

There would have been enough problems for the Muslim Turks with the figurative representation, let alone with this type of worship. In orthodox Islam, such behaviour would be categorized as *kaffir*, as heathen, as primitive, as totally unacceptable. The effects of these attitudes can be seen today in the former cathedral of Saint Sophia in Nicosia, which today bears the name of Selim, the Ottoman conqueror of the island.

Many years ago, virtually my first cultural experience of the Near East (the Middle East as we then called it) was taking the small train from the port of Famagusta to the capital, Nicosia. Soon after arriving I went down to that town to see its major monument, the fine Gothic cathedral built in the twelfth century as a result of the Crusaders' capture of the island in 1191. The outside of the building was a fine example of Western architecture of the period. But as I approached the west gate, I found everybody removing their shoes. For it had become a mosque, in which the atmosphere was totally different from that of a Christian place of worship. The walls and columns had been painted completely white, save for the capitals which were decorated in the primary reds, greens and yellows beloved in Islam. With the Turkish invasion of the island in 1570 and the defeat of the Catholic Venetians, the cathedral had followed the fate of Ayia Sophia in Istanbul and had been converted to Islamic use. The floor was covered in thick carpets and the whole orientation had been changed from east (towards Jerusalem) to south (towards Mecca). Above all there were no representations, no paintings, no sculpture; even abstract or geometrical design was virtually absent. What I realized only in 1999 when I returned to the island was that not only were there no statues in the exterior niches but the windows containing stained glass had been removed and replaced by an oriental-looking grille. Moreover, any figurative feature on the exterior of the building had been at least partly destroyed by being defaced. That also seems to have been the case with the gargoyles, which had been covered by aluminium spouts, probably because they too had been defaced and no longer worked.[2] All sculptured features around the building had been hammered with a heavy object, to destroy any imitative quality of living things they possessed. Mimesis was aberrant; representation was not only worthless, it was blasphemous.

The same contrast came to me in looking at the objects in the splendid Cyprus Museum in Nicosia, originally established as a memorial to the reign of Queen Victoria. Here the contrast was not between contemporary religions but over time. What was notable in the Neolithic collection is a groping towards the representation of humans and natural objects, which bursts out in the paintings on the pots of the Chalcolithic (Copper Age) period. Then suddenly we come to the Greek geometric phase, totally abstract in character, a feature that had extensive implications for the decorative arts in Cyprus. Later, with Ancient Greece, we find the vigorous and universal return of figurative representation, especially of the human form (which is also divine) – in other words, of three-dimensional sculpture. The changes are dramatic. Do they also represent the kind of ambivalence towards, doubts about, the very process of representation that we find in Plato and which I have recently discussed in a study, *Representations and Contradictions* (1997)? Not religious here but secular. I believe they do.

In any case the problems about representations are overtly demonstrated on the later Greek sculptures in Cyprus, for example, on those recovered from the famous site of Salamis. Very frequently the noses of these sculptures and in some cases the sexual features, the breasts or the testicles, have been damaged. But not in an accidental way. They have literally been defaced, denosed, castrated, presumably by incoming Muslims, who had continually been attacking the island since the early days of Islam and who eventually achieved political power with the Turkish conquest of 1571. After the establishment of British rule in 1878 a kind of balance was held between the two communities. Since independence, with a new political regime based on majority rule, the power position has changed again. The Greeks were always in the majority and in a democracy inevitably constituted the government, which was elected on communal rather than party lines. Moreover, it is an Orthodox government; their first leader was a priest, Makarios, and the president of the country is always attended by a priest on public occasions, making the dominant affiliation quite clear.

The two groups in contemporary Cyprus each have their own sacred and secular scripts, Greek in the first case, Arabic in the second, which ensures that they cannot read one another. But they also display strongly opposed ideologies, relating not simply to the obvious religious aspects of Christianity and Islam, but to all imagery of living things, a fact which sets them apart as far as objects in the world are concerned. And the world around them constantly reinforces this opposition, which is much more omnipresent than the notion of ethnicity or even of formal religion would suggest, leaving the opportunities for reconciliation thin and ineffective.

Ethnic cleansing

What has this got to do with 'ethnic cleansing'? Ethnic cleansing has become seen as a feature of the contemporary Balkans and as creating unspeakable horrors. It is nothing new on the face of the globe and it did not take nationalism or the nation-state to bring the process about. How else have most modern nations been formed? The expansion of Europe or Europeans throughout the world since the sixteenth century has involved constant movement, confinement and destruction, usually of 'primitive' peoples, throughout the Americas, in Australia, in South Africa, in the Caribbean, often turning autochthones into 'ethnic minorities', a process in which people of all races have been involved. Nor did the process begin with the modern world. How else did the Anglo-Saxons largely empty Great Britain of Celts, banishing them to the northern and western extremities? How else did the Latins move north into the German lands? Invasion is rarely a matter simply of establishing the elite; it also entails a new oppression of the earlier inhabitants.

More recently ethnic cleansing has been a dominant feature of the process of independence of the Indian sub-continent in 1947 and of the settlement of Jews (Israelis) in Arab Palestine, at least since the First World War. In both cases it involved Muslims and the members of another religion. That is a feature of the recent situation in Cyprus, and it has in fact marked the history of the whole of the Balkans since the Turks defeated the largely Slavic forces of the Christians. The coming of the Turks not only brought immigrant Muslims but also made many converts, although they risked savage punishment if this shift was found not to be 'genuine'. It was the Christians, even when numerically dominant, who became the underprivileged under Turkish rule. The encounter between these groups has led to long-term tensions in the region, not only with the dominant political and religious leadership at any historical moment but more especially with the arrival of democratic constitutions and ideologies, which stressed the question of the numerical strengths of one group relative to the other. That had not hitherto been the case.

Let us take the example of Kosovo, constantly in the forefront of contemporary attention. The majority of the population today is Albanian-speaking, yet the Serbs have been determined to hang on to the province and engaged, before and after the start of the recent NATO bombing and the departure of the Western observers, in driving the Albanians out of the territory. That province was granted autonomous status in Tito's Yugoslavia when the various groups had had in general fairly peaceful relations over the years, except during and following the German and Italian invasions in the course of the Second World War. Emphasis on nationalism, language and religion again came to the fore with the German recognition of an independent Slovenia soon after the fall of communism. That was the signal for the increased claims on ethnicity throughout the region, with the terrible consequences experienced by Bosnia, which could never become a unitary political regime, a nation, on these criteria. Kosovo followed; firstly the autonomous status was withdrawn because of the fear of encouraging claims for the independence of this sensitive province, then the Kosovans formed their own Liberation Army. The reaction of the Serbs to locally supported 'terrorism' was to threaten the population with expulsion.

The province is sensitive because it had been Serbian (first Ruscian) since the Nemanjid dynasty, whose borders included what are now Montenegro, Albania and Kosovo, and it was carved out in the twelfth century at the expense of the Byzantine Empire; though the Serbian Church became autocephalous, the ruler's son was crowned a Catholic, and the influence of Rome continued to grow in the area, especially in Croatia, although the founder remained Orthodox. The Orthodox Church continued to be very important in Serbia and Kosovo, and many early monasteries were established there, for example, near Novi Pazar. In the thirteenth century Peć in Kosovo became the seat of the archbishop. There were other reasons for the Slav presence too: the silver and other mines of Kosovo provided much of the wealth of the medieval Serbian kingdom.

It was in Kosovo that the Serbian Empire, which included Macedonia and parts of Greece, was defeated by the Turks in June 1389 at Kosovo Polje, 'the Field of the Blackbirds', near Prishtina, where their prince, Lazar, met his death (was 'martyred'). As a result of this defeat the Muslim Turks became masters of much of the Balkans, introducing Islam into the whole area, especially the towns, through immigration and conversion. As we have seen, the Turks were invaders from Central Asia who had allied themselves with the Seljuks, the masters of the Abbasid caliphate of Baghdad, and then occupied Anatolia on the borders of the Byzantine Empire. Profiting from internal quarrels among the Christian powers, the Ottoman Turks established themselves at Gallipoli, long before the fall of Constantinople in 1453, entering Europe in 1354. They sent troops to Thrace and were caught up in the Balkan conflicts between the Alains, Christianized Turks, Greeks, Almogavares (Catalan mercenaries) and Slavs. From then on they constituted an important force in Eastern Europe, where Austria, Hungary, Poland and Lithuania were also major players. The attempt of the Serbs to establish their own empire replacing Byzantium came to nothing when after some initial successes the kings of Serbia and of Bosnia were defeated, together with their allies from the West, probably including Albanians, by the Sultan Murad I, who had his own Christian vassals. The Turkish advance into Europe ended 300 years later with the Ottoman–Hapsburg war of 1662–9, leading to an attack upon and then the relief of Vienna, said to have been celebrated by the invention of the croissant, representing the defeat of the pincer movement of Islam. In 1688 Belgrade was taken and the Austrian troops went on to attempt to expel the Turks, when the Serbs of Kosovo rose up against their rulers. But with calls on their army for the religious wars in Germany, the Austrians were forced to retire, taking with them in the 'Great Migration' the patriarch of Peć and 37,000 Serbian families to the present-day Vojvodina. Kosovo, the centre of the Serbian Empire, now became the goal of immigration by Albanian Muslims who continued to live under Turkish rule, even when Serbia itself had been liberated. That province was only united with Serbia as the result of the Balkan wars of 1912–13.

The numbers of people involved in the Great Migration are open to question. But with the retaking of Belgrade by the Turks, some 40,000 then fled to Hungary. Otherwise only a few hundred in that city escaped being killed. One commentator notes: 'the country and its people were indeed destroyed, massacred by the barbarians, and enslaved' (Malcolm 1998: 158). The English agent at Edine thought the province would never recover.

In these struggles the religious aspect was often to the fore. An inhabitant of Prishtina reported that his uncle, the archbishop, already dead, was dug up 'and put out as food for the dogs in the middle of the square, with his mitre on his head' (Malcolm 1998: 157), thus stressing the role of religion in the conflict. After the war had ended, the Ottomans maintained 'their hostility and suspicions towards their Christian subjects' (Malcolm 1998: 164). For two decades after 1690 'a new wave of Islamicization seems to have taken place', 'using conversion as a pacification measure', as well as heavier taxation, to force conversion or exile. Many priests were killed in the course of these struggles.

In 1737 a further Austrian advance was followed by a retreat leading to the Second Migration, which included refugees from the Prishtina region. Following this withdrawal there was a steady flow of Albanians into Kosovo during these years (Malcolm 1998: 173), some of whom were converts. 'Not until late in the nineteenth century would the major town of Kosovo recover the population levels they had enjoyed before 1690' (Malcolm 1998: 177), during which time the dervish orders expanded their activities considerably, extending and consolidating Islam.

Kosovo became a largely Muslim province of the Ottoman Empire, though some Catholic clans remained in the Albanian mountains. It was subject to some colonization by Turks as well as by Circassians from the Caucasus, but in the towns the Muslim population increased mainly through economic conversion (Malcolm 1998: 107); conversion meant that taxes were immediately reduced. So the country became and remained strongly Muslim; indeed, even during the revolts and rebellions at the beginning of the nineteenth century, the ordinary Albanians stayed loyal to the Ottoman Empire (Malcolm 1998: 246). Later the traditionalists struggled, even against the Young Turks, for the maintenance of the sharia (the religious law) and of the old Arabic script rather than adopting the 'alien' Roman one.

With the founding of Yugoslavia after the First World War, a main object of the Serbian monarchy was to re-establish the ethnic and demographic equilibrium in the province. Some Serbian colonization took place, encouraged by certain British and American charities. The Serbian intention was

117

to secure an outlet to the Adriatic, but this aim had been frustrated by Austrian interests, who insisted on the creation of an independent Albania. Soldiers were resettled to recolonize the 'Holy Land', and many Albanians left Kosovo with the Turks for Turkey. Nevertheless the political party representing local concerns was significantly called the Islamic Association for the Defence of Justice (Malcolm 1998: 269), which aimed not only to maintain the sharia but also the *waqf*, the bey's feudal estates, as well as the maternal language. So successful was the process of resettlement that in 1929 Serbs and Montenegrins constituted 61 per cent of the population.

In the Second World War, the reverse happened. The Albanians of the area welcomed the Italian invaders in April 1939 as a way of opposing the Serbs, and the Italians then included Kosovo in a Greater Albania, allowing the population to be educated in their own language. Some 100,000 Serbs fled northwards to Serbia, which continued to engage in a very vigorous struggle against the Axis forces. With the end of the war in 1945 the situation was once again reversed, and the Serbs attempted to re-establish their demographic position. However, in 1974 the province was given an autonomous status by Tito because, by 1971, 73.7 per cent were Albanians. Autonomy included the re-establishment of their own schools. Soon after the death of Tito in 1981 the Albanians rose up demanding independence, leading many Serbs to leave the area, and many more to regret the earlier granting of autonomy. By 1991 the Serbs were only 11 per cent of the population. Nevertheless in 1989 Serbia decided to celebrate there the 600th anniversary of the Field of the Blackbirds. Worried about its indeterminate boundaries, it suppressed the autonomy of the province, encouraging the Kosovans to take to guerrilla warfare,[3] in fact engaging in a civil war led by the Maoist-inspired Kosovan Liberation Army (Albania was Maoist China's one ally). This group was at one time listed by the USA as a 'terrorist' organization but was later transformed into an ally. The USA became increasingly willing to recognize the territory as autonomous, though that was not included in the original aims of the recent war and such a project clearly runs counter to earlier UN policy regarding non-interference in the internal affairs of its member states.

The conflicts have continued after attempts by the NATO forces to stop ethnic cleansing. Many Serbs left Kosovo when the Albanians poured in; others were molested and forced out. Even a convoy under NATO protection taking Serbs from Montenegro was attacked in Peć, the excuse given by the Albanian authorities being that this incident was in revenge for Serb atrocities during the war.[4] Understandable, but such tit-for-tat has to be seen in the context of a continuing feuding situation between the two parties over a very long period, not unlike the feuding situations between Albanian clans described by Margaret Hasluck in the 1930s (Hasluck 1954). The opposition between Muslim Albanians and Orthodox Serbs persists today. The situation at the border area of Mitrovica was not simply a problem created by Slobodan Milosević. The stones were being thrown by angry Serbs who resented the powers acquired by equally angry neighbours. To create a foreign policy, let alone fight a war, in the belief that, by ridding the country of one man – as the USA believed in the voices of Albright and Clinton – one can solve the problem is completely to misinterpret a thousand years of Balkan history. The same can be said for the problem of Saddam Hussein and the voices of Rumsfeld and Bush.

There are two problems with the notion of ethnic cleansing: the first has to do with ethnicity, the second with cleansing. Ethnic is a description that has been adopted in a blanket fashion to refer to any large grouping with some semblance of cultural homogeneity, often in a subordinate position. Cleansing is a process of consolidation in which every nation-state has been involved. The Anglo-Saxons did it to the Celts, as the Celts had done to the Picts.

The concept of ethnicity has been widely taken up in the social sciences, since it gets around the problem of defining the distinctive character of the unity of the people in question (that is, an ethnos, the presumed subject of ethnology). Was it based on language, religion, common origin or culture in some vague sense of that word? Ethnicity covers all as well as covering up all. Moreover, it implies differences of a primordial kind, ones you cannot shake off. In the present case its use seems to disguise the specific role of religion in many such situations.

A similar conclusion is reached in the account of the neighbouring Bosnia by Sells, who comes from a Serbian-American family. He writes: 'The word "ethnic" in "ethnic cleansing" is a euphemism. Bosnians, Serbs, Croats and Muslims all speak the same language' (Sells 1996: 13). Later:

> They are divided only by religious criteria. Those organis-ing the persecution identified themselves through explicit religious symbols, such as the three-figured hand gestures representing the Christian Trinity, the images of sacred figures of Serbian religious mythology on their uniform insignia, the songs they memorised and forced their victims to sing, the priest's ring they kissed before and after their acts of per-secution, and the formal religious ceremonies. (Sells 1996: 15)

The attacks on Muslims in Bosnia came of course from both Catholic Croatian and Orthodox Serbian groups, who had at one time the common aim to split Bosnia between them-selves and eliminate the Muslim element. Tudjman's policy of 'Europeanization' meant exactly this. Other attacks have to be seen in the context of the religious struggle between the Catholic West and the Orthodox East, just as yet others are linked to the Catholic–Protestant split; above all it is the Christian–Muslim opposition that affected not only Cyprus and the Balkans but the whole of the Near East, North Africa and Mediterranean Europe. As in Cyprus, this has to be seen in the context of the struggle (for 'freedom') against Ottoman domination – Muslims are still often known as Turks in the Balkans. In Bosnia some Croats and Serbs believed the Muslims intended to establish an Islamic republic, which some of them were said to have expressed as an aim. The recruitment of mujahedin fighters from Asia gave some colour to this claim. Past experiences made matters worse. In the Second World War two SS divisions had been formed from Kosovo Albanians, though others fought on the allied side. More threateningly, the Muslims were also feared because of their higher birthrate; Albanian women were described as 'breeding machines'. This religious opposition led to the wholesale destruction of mosques on the one side and of churches on the other. The fear was mutual. In 1987, 60,000 Serbs signed a petition condemning the 'fascist genocide' in Kosovo (Sells 1996: 58). The Serbian Orthodox bishops made a declaration about genocide in Kosovo, where the Albanians were perceived as trying to create an 'ethnically pure' state. It was not only extremists who were worried; in 1986 a group of Belgrade intellectuals prepared a 'Serbian Memorandum' for restructuring the relations of Kosovo to Serbia, to prevent what they called the 'Crucifixion' of the Serb nation.

As with many of the earlier examples of so-called ethnic cleansing, the problem here centres upon a religious difference – as in the case of Hinduism and Islam in India, of Jews and Arabs in Palestine, of Jews and Christians in the European holocaust. In that sense the problems are hardly 'ethnic', an epithet that often tends to conceal the true state of affairs (Eagleton 1999). The troubles in Northern Ireland are basically religious. And while they have not reached the point of ethnic cleansing, it is at least arguable that, as with the division of Ireland that set up the Free State, a separation of the groups involved, conducted if possible under more favourable circumstances and supervised by outsiders rather than left to the participants themselves, might be a practical solution to continuing conflict.

The separation of the parties to a continuous conflict is a potential choice in a number of circumstances and cannot be universally condemned. Where that course is condemned and attempts are envisaged to reverse the cleansing, there is often a problem of who was originally where. That has been the case in Kosovo and in Cyprus. It may therefore be virtually impossible to reverse the results of ethnic cleansing, notably in the examples of Israel and India, even when it is possible to come to some conclusion about who belongs where. How long does it take, what majority does it take, to decide that the Australian Aborigines or the native Americans are entitled or not to have their cleansing reversed? If one made such an attempt in Kosovo, should one re-establish the situation that existed in 1998, 1991, 1929 or even before the coming of the Muslims? Delicate ethical issues are involved. The same ethical considerations apply to Israel's occupation of the West Bank. Clearly, in practice, reversal very much depends upon the respective power of the contesting parties.

Ethnic cleansing then has always been around in the sense that people have driven out others in taking possession of a territory. To condemn it out of hand is to condemn ourselves, or our past selves whom we would not wish to have to rehabilitate. Moreover, the nature of this cleansing is often viewed very differently by the two parties involved. What the Ottomans saw in 1925 as the return of the Greeks to their motherland from Turkish soil, the Greeks see as their expulsion by invaders of their ancient homeland. It may be that they arrived many centuries ago from the other side of the Aegean, but they had been there a long time and established a remarkable civilization on the Ionian coast. The Turks too see themselves as having occupied Anatolia for over 500 years. Islam and Christianity are not merely symbolic of this ethnic difference but the very constituents of it. Both have fought wars to establish themselves, the Greeks their war of independence in 1821, the Turks their earlier struggles of conquest and later ones to hold back the Christian forces.

My second point has to do with the ethnic component of this cleansing. Ethnic and ethnicity have become cant words in the social sciences and often in everyday speech. As I have suggested, the usage is very often undefined and employed in a blanket fashion. In many of the cases to which

I have referred, the ethnic elements have been minimal; often enough what are linguistically, and in many respects culturally, the same basic groups are involved in an internecine struggle – in Ireland, for example, or in the conflicts among the Semitic-speaking peoples. One common thread throughout (not the only one but nevertheless very important) has been a struggle between members of different religious congregations rather than between those displaying differences of a 'national', 'racial' or 'ethnic' character. Such non-religious differences may certainly be relevant in other cases; in Belgium it was language (after the earlier religious split with the Dutch).

Another line of thinking, not only Marxist, identified such conflicts with 'class' and 'oppression'. But neither in Yugoslavia nor in Cyprus is it primarily a class conflict, although elements of stratification were inevitably involved in the political dominance of one group over another. In Cyprus the Turks provided many of the administrative and legal personnel, even after the British took over in 1878. In the Balkans, Muslims often dominated the towns and formed the merchant class. But essentially the division in both areas ran along religious lines. In Southern and Eastern Europe that division had to do with the westward expansion of Islam into the continent, by the Arabs in the South and spearheaded by the Turks in the East; however, the former were expelled from Spain, Sicily and Malta by the *reconquista* of the fifteenth century, in itself a kind of cleansing process (and culminating in the clearing out of Jews as well as of Muslims). Of course people convert from one religion to another for economic or political reasons, as we have seen in Kosovo. Conversion is a feature of all (written) world religions. And conversions of this kind happened in Hindu India to Islam, to Christianity and more recently to Buddhism, often involving the lower castes. But once the conversion has taken place the religion is no longer an expression of, say, class; its ideology, its world view, its practices and beliefs take over as autonomous factors and may in turn provide or support what is often spoken of as ethnic identity.

Religious affiliation, despite the possibility of conversion, is more 'primordial' than nationality. Moving to America, Germans, Italians and English become citizens of the United States and lose their nationality; even 'origins' are of rather marginal importance in most cases (except perhaps for the Irish). But Jews remain Jews, Catholics remain Catholics, and Muslims Muslims. Centuries of persecution in Europe did not persuade most Jews to renounce their faith. And those who did were always regarded as potential renegades. The mythical themes of ritual murder by Jews and of cannibalism by Christians point to the fact that one is dealing with conflicts stemming from a more potent level of reality than nationalism, one where no surrender is possible, where there are no prisoners of war.

The descendants of Scots who first migrated from Ireland to Scotland in the Dalriadic invasions of the Dark Ages later returned to the north of Ireland. But their 'ethnic' identity differs from that of the southern Irish only on religious grounds; they are Protestant, the others Catholic. The same kind of sectarian religious division took place throughout Europe with Huguenots, Calvinists and Lutherans; it happened in Islam with Sunnis and Shiites, and in India with Jains, Buddhists and Hindus.

The sweeping autonomy of religion is epitomized in architecture throughout the Mediterranean. The 'Moorish style' largely excludes figurative representation on theological grounds, and concentrates upon geometric and abstract forms. Such an architecture spread from the Near East, with the magnificent Mosque of Lutfullah in the Persian city of Isfahan, westwards to the extraordinary Alhambra palace of Granada, eastwards to the Taj Mahal in India and beyond. Virtually nothing figurative made its appearance, except in secular Persian and Mughal art. Such world-wide and world-shattering designs of an abstract kind are not 'expressions' of ethnicity, or politics, or the economy, except in a very limited sense. They are the manifestations, the outcome, of an aniconic religious system which has very important political and social features and equally significant consequences.

Bitter Icons and Ethnic Cleansing

As Daniel emphasizes in his book on European–Arab relations during the Middle Ages (1975), there was in many ways a great deal of commonality between the two parties. But they were divided over religion, and the norms of religion entailed differences over politics, kinship, the family, and many other areas. That is what the historian Guichard was referring to when he wrote of 'structures occidentales' and 'structures orientales' in Andalusia before 1472, the year that saw the end of the kingdom of Granada. Typically, Spanish historiography, especially under the fascist General Franco, had played down the Islamic contribution to Iberian life. Spain's achievements were seen as Christian European achievements. In fact since the end of the eighth century, Spain had provided a bridgehead between East and West, or more accurately perhaps between South and North or between Islam and Christianity, with profound effects for Europe in the later Middle Ages leading up to the Renaissance, to which these contacts contributed.

There was considerable communication between Europeans and Arabs, but it was mainly when they acted as Christians and Muslims that problems arose. So poets on either side were largely spared. We hear of the killing of Arabs learned in the religious law, but not of those who were more learned in secular accomplishments (Daniel 1975: 105). In the secular world there were fewer barriers between the two sides. Take the love poetry of the troubadours which Europeans often see as characteristically theirs. Daniel compares the courtly poetry of Provençal with that of the small courts of the *muluk at-tawaif*, the petty Arab kings of the eleventh century. He writes:

> On the whole, it seems undeniable that courtly poetry in Arabic, often trivial, yet ranged much more widely in theme and treatment than troubadour verse. If the latter had not a special position in European literary history, it might be well regarded as no more than a provincial and decadent offshoot of the court poets of Spain . . . If, however, European concepts of courtly love derive from the petty courts of the taifas

125

(which appeared when the Caliphate collapsed in 1031), the whole romantic tradition in European literature owes an almost disproportionate debt to eleventh-century Spain. It has been argued that there is evidence of Platonic ideas in Provence at this period, conjectured to derive from Ibn Hazm. (Daniel 1975: 105–6)

Even Nelli, a French historian of the troubadours and of the Cathars, sees the romantic tradition, the refraining from intimate sexual acts, the man's subordination to the lady, as deriving not only from Arabic but from Byzantine and other sources. 'All Nelli's possibilities', comments Daniel, 'suggest the ambiguity or multiplicity of the origin of European romanticism' (Daniel 1975: 106–7).

Certainly Moorish Spain was very significant, as the mention of Ibn Hazm suggests. The author wrote *The Ring of the Dove* (1022), a poem about the art of love. But while that work was certainly composed in Spain, and therefore European in a geographical sense, historians from the north have often drawn a boundary south of the Pyrenees that excludes influences from the Arab kingdoms from consideration, concentrating upon developments north of that line. As Daniel's account makes clear, from the standpoint of literature that is the wrong boundary. What is European has become identified with what is (specifically) Christian.

Members of different religious groups have lived together in the Mediterranean region over very long periods, and while there has been much interaction, there has also often been the potentiality for discord if not always for open conflict. There was a constant shift between rejection and a qualified acceptance. The former took the shape of pogroms which were a constant feature of the European landscape. But at the same time the Jews, for example, played an important role as merchants, as shopkeepers and as bankers. Assimilation with the dominant religious culture meant the possibility of apostasy or the total neglect of one's previous religious affiliations, and even this renunciation did not always help since the fear of a return to that earlier faith was

Bitter Icons and Ethnic Cleansing

always present, as with former Christians in Moorish Spain, or converted Jews in the rest of Europe. Daniel writes: 'there has often been ill-feeling between Christendom and Islam, but there has never perhaps been greater hatred than that which those Christians that supported the Martyrs' movement felt in Cordoba in the ninth century' (Daniel 1975: 23). These martyrs deliberately sought their own destruction by going out of their way to proclaim their faith and to insist that the dominant Islam was wrong, was evil. For these men and women, whom Daniel describes as fanatics, there was no compromise, no understanding of another creed. They represented one continuing theme in medieval Christianity that led Spain to expel the Moriscos, then the Jews, as well as to establish the Inquisition. 'Christianity cannot exist side-by-side with any other religion' (Daniel 1975: 48), it was said. In the mirror image of Nicosia, Cordoba has installed a church within a mosque.

In the West this opposition between Christianity and Islam has led to a general devaluation of the contributions of Arab and, more broadly, Islamic culture to European achievements. There has been some acknowledgement of their discoveries in the scientific sphere where European scholarship has long recognized the debt of the Renaissance to Arab translators of classical sources, though there is still a good deal of equivocation on certain points, for example, on the debt of the schools of medicine at Salerno and Montpellier to Arab sources.

From the twelfth century onwards, some technological developments were shared; for example, the windmill, the mariner's compass, the trebuchet, guns and gunpowder, the mechanical clock. The history of the development of these is not always certain, but there was at least a profitable interchange of experience, so that each side was at once creditor and debtor to the other . . . Only later did Europe draw ahead. (Daniel 1975: 309)

Yet Europeans frequently view these developments as specifically their own, as was the case with love. European

127

civilization is often counted as essentially Christian by historians and sociologists alike, despite the contribution made by Muslims and Jews in the past and the presence of these communities within its boundaries (Gabrieli 1983).

The struggle between Christians and Muslims ('Arabs', 'Moors') became a matter of extermination as the latter were expelled from Spain and Italy. Daniel concludes: 'we have seen how the moral identity of Europe was preserved by a fiercely determined orthodoxy which wanted nothing to do with any least deviation in the whole field of religion, and how religion itself became the expression of that same sense of identity' (Daniel 1975: 303). It seems doubtful if one should regard religion as an *expression* of identity; that appears to me to smack of sociological mysticism. Rather it is in itself a major factor in differentiation, in the very establishment of identity. That is the case in Serbia too. Of that country Malcolm writes: 'When modern concepts of nationhood began to be propagated in the nineteenth century, membership of this church supplied a ready-made "category of Serbianism"' (Malcolm 1998: 12). What is remarkable about the whole of the former USSR is the revival of religious affiliation, in the Caucasus in the East, in Russia itself, after fifty years of communism which tried to repress such beliefs. Religion is not an expression or a handle so much as a major constituent of such identity. In East Timor it is the Catholic Church in an otherwise Muslim land (except for Hindu Bali) that makes them what they are, as we see each day with images of the bishop's palace, of churches destroyed, of people crossing themselves before a statue of the Virgin Mary, an act that is anathema to any iconophobic Muslim.

Why should religion be such a potent factor behind these conflicts? To give it so great an importance runs contrary to the largely secular ideologies under which the West now lives, secular ideologies which inspired Atatürk in Turkey and Nehru in India. But to mention those countries is to remind ourselves of the persistence of the religious factor; Turkey now has a Muslim government, India a Hindu one.

That situation brings out one main difference with racial and linguistic factors; religious ones can be eliminated not only by 'cleansing' and expulsion but also by conversion, which leaves other primordial features in place but replaces the ideology as well as the institutions. Does that very possibility call for greater defensive measures on the actors' part, a more fundamentalist reaction?

Religious roots, though not thought of as 'primordial' in the same way as nationality, and as always subject to the possibility of conversion or of apathy, are nevertheless of a very long-enduring kind. To some extent, the American Jewish community has never become fully American, if by that is meant 'only' American, since it gives strong support to another state that defines itself as Jewish, that is the state of Israel. The community has itself provided not only immense funds to that state but also many immigrants, the result of which has led to changes in the practice if not the law of nationality (permitting dual nationality) and has strongly influenced American foreign policy. That situation may well provide the model for the future accommodation and political action of Muslim communities in Europe, rather than the way that national groups of French, British, Germans and other immigrants have been incorporated in the United States. Religious accommodation is *sui generis*.

At the ideological level religion penetrates and divides. To believe in one God is to exclude the many. In some religions, in particular those originating in the Near East, such beliefs link the individual directly with the Creator of his or her world and hence with the sources of its pleasure and its pain. That link with the Creator God obviously relates to the very creation of our world and our species, to our present existence and to our future after death. Methods of worshipping divinity (of crossing one's self, the wearing of hats, the position of the hands, of the posture of the body generally), approaches to representation, divide communities in radical ways (we know the correct way, they do not) and ones that are likely to be brought to the fore in threatening times. Across that divide the Greek Cypriots threatened the

Turks with the prospect of enosis, union with Greece; the
Turks replied with forces from the mainland. The Kosovo
Albanians threatened the Orthodox Serbs with taking control of their holy and sacred places, not only the Field of the
Blackbirds but also the ancient Orthodox monasteries built
in the area; the Serbs replied by trying to chase out not only
the Liberation Army but the population as a whole. Not
simply at the theological level but in worship and in daily
affairs, religion divides in a way that leads readily to the
demonization of opponents. Of that the West is reminded
in the earlier relations between Protestants and Catholics,
resulting in attempts by one to eliminate the other, a bloody
struggle that still continues in Northern Ireland; even in
England the situation is remembered, indeed celebrated,
annually in the popular bonfire ceremonies of Guy Fawkes,
a reminder of the times when opponents were indeed burnt
at the stake.

Religion and political science

Much of the interesting discussion about nationality and
nationalism, for example in the works of Gellner (1983)
and Hobsbawm (1990), has tended to look for transcultural
factors in their rise and establishment. They are certainly
correct in seeing the universalization of the notion of the
nation-state, those units into which the whole world is now
divided, for example by the League of Nations, or more
recently by the United Nations, as a modern phenomenon,
promoted from the top. But the bases on which such units
emerge and are formed seem to be plural and not at all
unitary. They may relate to language or territory, but one very
significant dimension, neglected in the post-Enlightenment
of Western intellectuals that has promoted secularization
and scepticism, is the ideological factor associated with religious beliefs.

It was not only the Enlightenment that changed things. It
has also been ideas about the role of religion in modernization.

In the late Victorian Age Sir James Frazer, the author of *The Golden Bough*, saw magic as giving way to religion and then to science. The whole development was layered like the geological strata on which notions of evolution were based. Modern man paid only marginal attention to religion. That was true of the approaches of the socialist Eric Hobsbawm, the agnostic Ernst Gellner and the 'modernist' Anthony Giddens. But it simply is not true, except among intellectuals. Certainly, church attendance in Europe has fallen, but many are now attached to less orthodox factions. In some countries such as Poland the pull of religion is as strong as ever while in others it remains a defining feature at a very general level, waiting to come to the surface under crisis conditions, when for example 'our Christian civilization' or Jewish culture or Muslim way of life is threatened. We may neglect or even set aside religion; we would not abandon the religious epithet, let alone the associated values and ceremonies.

It is notable that the maps at the end of Hobsbawm's admirable book *Nations and Nationalism since 1780* (1990) include 'nationalities', peoples, languages, political divisions, but not religions. Gellner suggests that, 'Among cultures, it is the ones linked to a high (literate) faith which seem most likely to fill the role of crystallizer of discontent' (1983: 74). That remark again seems to me typical of an approach that sees religion as dependent upon other more profound factors (here that of discontent). I would argue that religion must be taken as a primary element of identities in this context.

In a more complex manner the same caveat applies to Halliday's analysis of politics in the Near East (1995), where he begins by distinguishing between (religious) Islam and (secular) 'Islam', and goes on to set aside the religious version. He writes that 'Islam' is a 'social and political system', Islam is 'a religion, espousing certain clear doctrines', which 'exists as a system of belief about the supernatural and related questions of morality, destiny and meaning. This is a matter for believers and theologians and is not the subject of what follows' – that is, his political analysis (1995: 2). For the reasons I have outlined, that dismissal is neither possible nor desirable. I disagree profoundly with a division which seems to me to be explicitly repudiated by Halliday's dedication of the book to 'Iranian friends and democrats, opponents of the religiously sanctioned dictatorship'. The reasoning behind an approach which sets aside the religious is that we have difficulty in understanding how others could invest so significantly in beliefs when we cannot. Consequently we downgrade these beliefs, and the associated icons become objects of art or of 'material culture' rather than critical constituents of faith. To Western intellectuals such prejudices are the bequest of the Enlightenment and of subsequent secularization.

My argument is that still today 'ethnic cleansing', which has been fundamental in the creation of many nations, is in some (but not all) cases strongly motivated by religious factors. Such influences are not confined to the theological aspects but penetrate into the way we represent the material and consequently the immaterial, the spiritual, worlds. These factors may be reduced, as when advanced capitalism provides alternative goals, as in the United States, or when communism does the same, for instance, formerly in Eastern Europe. But even in the socialist countries, as has happened in Turkey and India, we have seen religious factors re-emerge in dramatic ways, and, while antagonisms remain less strong in the prosperous, consumer-oriented, money-making environment of the USA, religious values are certainly significant in that country and have taken violent as well as peaceful forms. Although they may still be so central in the modern world, an appreciation of religious factors has often been neglected by recent European historians, sociologists and political scientists alike, who have been reared in the sceptical and secular traditions of the Enlightenment. Current political problems in the Balkans, in Ireland, in Timor, and now elsewhere in Indonesia, in India, in Egypt and in Nigeria, should lead to a radical reconsideration of these views.

3

Islam and Terrorism

In recent days terrorism has been linked to Islam, and, as we have seen, the political-religious nature of Muslim governments meant that there was an association between the sword and the crescent that was different from that between the cross and the musket. But of course all our pasts have been scattered with those who have resorted to unauthorized force and unconventional tactics, the Robin Hoods, the bandits and the primitive rebels. These have indeed been our heroes, even though they might now be classified as 'terrorists', a term first applied to the Jacobins in the French Revolution. The word crops up frequently in the struggles between Islamic and Christian groups that I discussed in the previous chapter; what is to one side a terrorist is to the other a freedom fighter. Both become legitimate if they seize power. But the word is used in many other situations for those who resisted the dominance of the state with its over-riding claim to the monopoly of force. Anybody else was constrained to use other means to assert themselves, especially if the state did not permit opposition. That was true of all fascist regimes, and indeed of other totalitarian ones such as the Soviet Union, although in the latter case protesters tended to be identified as 'counter-revolutionaries'. The most extreme case was perhaps that of Palestine in the 1930s, where the Jews were fighting the government of the mandated territory over the policy of restricted immigration, at the same time as opposing the Arabs who thought even the restricted immigration too threatening. Eventually the Jewish terrorists, with heavy help from outside, especially from the USA, defeated the Arabs and established the state of Israel in 1948. The terrorists then became the legitimate government. The new terrorists were the Muslims who had lost control of the country.

The dilemma is particularly clear in the contemporary conflict between India and Pakistan over Kashmir. That country is largely Muslim and the majority are opposed to India and would probably opt for independence. Those fighting for freedom are characterized as 'terrorists' by India and by the USA, but for Pakistan the situation is more complex. The Pakistanis were led to condemn the Afghan Taliban as terrorist by the USA, who had earlier supported that group as freedom fighters in their struggle against Soviet occupation. Now similar groups are struggling against India, with Pakistani support. So that the leader of Pakistan is forced to condemn their methods as terrorist to get international support, especially American, while agreeing with their aims. But what alternative methods do they have to pursue those aims in the face of the armed power of the state?

A different version of this process occurred in many colonial territories in the struggle for independence. Some of the later leaders of these countries had spent time in prison, and, if they were not considered terrorists, they were certainly seen to be involved in illegal or illegitimate political activity that sometimes included violence. That was true not only of the Irgun Leumi in Palestine, an underground terrorist organization, one of whose leaders, Begin, eventually became prime minister. It was also true in Cyprus, where Archbishop Makarios was viewed as having connections with the local Greek fighters, illegal of course, who were struggling for enosis, union with Greece, and at the time engaged in killing British soldiers. He later became the first prime minister. So too with many of the leaders of the ANC in

South Africa, some of whom, like Mandela, spent long years in prison because of their association with illegal armed force. The same was the case in Zimbabwe and perhaps in Kenya, with Kenyatta's connections with the Mau Mau. Since these nationalist movements were faced with the forces of the colonial state (the forces of 'law and order') from which they felt themselves excluded, the resort to 'terrorist' activities, to guerilla warfare, was the only way they felt they could make themselves heard. There was of course a Third Way, namely the resort to civil disobedience on a massive scale, a policy successfully practised in a few colonial situations. Such a programme was most explicitly developed in the approach of Mahatma Gandhi with his doctrine of *ahimsa*, or non-violence, epitomized in the Salt March of 1930 and in his hunger strikes against British rule. But, by and large, such tactics have not been seen as an option for most opposition movements that have opposed the power of the state. So that they felt they had to resort to force of an illegitimate kind, including terrorism.

According to lawyers specializing in the law of war, what distinguishes the illegal fighter, including 'the partisan and the guerrilla, but especially the terrorist', is that they 'exploit the benefits of stealth and surprise and so deny an opponent fair warning that they are on a mission of war.'[1] But rebel groups are hardly in a position to carry on their activities and to give their opponents warning of their attacks.

Does a pre-emptive strike fall within the category of the use of illegal force? In 1981 the Israelis made a pre-emptive strike on an Iraqi factory being built by the French and alleged to be making nuclear material. In 1998 the USA took out a factory in the Sudan said to have been making material for chemical weapons, about which some doubt has been expressed. What is the position in international law? How are these different from the pre-emptive strike of the Japanese on Hawaii in 1942, or of the German invasion of various countries in the 1930s? In all cases stealth and surprise were involved.

Clearly one factor would be the intention of the party attacked and its capability of being a threat. Sudan may have been a threat in that for a time it harboured Bin Laden, who was in the business of attacking American installations. It is difficult to see the difference objectively between that and the harbouring of IRA fundraisers and others by the USA. That hardly gives the right for Britain to bomb targets in the USA, quite apart from considerations of dominant force. Was not Saddam entitled, from an Arab point of view, to see the Israelis as a threat to Arab lands, in the West Bank, in Jerusalem and even in Israel itself? Should he therefore be permitted to take out Israeli means of mass destruction, such as nuclear plants?

In describing opponents as terrorists, no effort is made to consider their political or religious agenda. They are the enemy, who resort to violence for violence's sake. They kill and maim our people and destroy our property. But nonetheless ideological agendas are usually present. The Catholic IRA does not kill for the sake of killing; it has been trying to expel the British and establish a united Ireland. Unfortunately for them, the presence of larger numbers of Protestants in the North has prevented them achieving this aim. Equally, Islamic movements such as al-Qaeda aim to reduce the influence of the USA and other Western powers, especially on Near Eastern affairs, forcing them to remove their military forces from the region (in particular from the Holy Land of Arabia) and to permit the creation of a Palestinian state. Indeed they would like to create states ruled according to Islamic law throughout the region, perhaps united into a larger unit, the better to treat with those they see as oppressing them.

Not simply oppressing them but imposing their culture upon them, hence their defiance of some aspects of 'modernization'. For instance, the tourist trade has undoubtedly benefited many countries economically. Young people from the West have flocked on cheap holidays to sunny climates, where they have drunk their own drinks, eaten their own food, danced, swum, gambled and generally had fun. That is not how it appears to many Muslims, who see these resorts as excrescences on their landscape, because of the breaking of many of the prohibitions of Muslim society regarding drink, food, sexual behaviour and in other ways. The insouciance of the Western youth often gives deep offence to such people, quite apart from emphasizing the great gap that exists between 'them', the rich, and 'us', the poor. Like the Twin Towers, the massacre in Bali was a terrible tragedy for the West, but for some in the East it was comparable to God's punishment of the Sodomites. And to understand more clearly that kind of motivation we have only to think of the attitudes of New England Puritans, of European conquerors of the American Indians or of fighters against the Moors and Turks who thought the enemy deserved whatever fate God meted out for their sins, even their total destruction.[2]

One widespread situation in which terrorism came to the fore as guerrilla warfare was in resisting the occupation of one's territory by enemy forces. Clearly these latter had gained the dominant position by defeating the legitimate military forces of the country concerned so the only possible way of expressing one's opposition, and ultimately of bringing that occupation to an end (though that end was rarely achieved by resistance forces alone), was by attacking the occupying army by violent means (such as happened throughout occupied Europe towards the end of the Second World War). Such 'resistance' is inevitably seen as 'terrorism' by the occupying forces, who have great difficulties in dealing with such tactics and have often themselves resorted to 'terrorist' tactics, such as rounding up and possibly shooting some of the civilian population who may have had little or nothing to do with the actual violence. Examples of such activities were found frequently in occupied Europe, in France, Italy and in most of the other countries. The massacres of Oradour in France and of the Ardeatine caves near Rome were cases in point. It was also characteristic of the Balkans, where Tito led an effective 'terrorist' force from the mountainous areas against the occupying Axis powers. He too became the first leader of the post-war republic of Yugoslavia. More

137

recently, Kosovan 'terrorism' has subsequently been legitimized because it achieved victory, following Western support; its leaders and its followers have become incorporated in a newly autonomous area. The 'Albanian' population in Macedonia then took up similar tactics but have failed to secure similar support or similar ends, though they have made some political gains. They remain 'terrorists'.

There is another situation in which the word 'terrorist' has often been employed in relation to the character of the victims of an attack rather than its legality, that is, when those victims are unarmed civilians, especially women and children, rather than 'soldiers'. In earlier times the distinction had perhaps greater validity, but modern warfare, conducted at a distance, often from the air, is no respecter of the difference between armed and unarmed. Moreover it could well be argued that, where an invading force includes women and children, as initially in the USA or as in most colonization, all were proper targets for resistance fighters.

That claim was made in wartime Europe and again in Palestine today. There is a further aspect to so-called terrorism, when this consists of acts of violence, assassinations, carried out against leaders or office-holders, where the action is broadly symbolic, such as the recent shooting of the Dutch right-wing leader Pim Fortuyn, or of the British minister of state in Cairo by the Irgun Leumi in 1944, in Tsarist Russia or in many other examples from South America. 'Propaganda by the deed', in the anarchist's phrase, is denounced by most politicians as being ineffective, an individual protest rather than a collective action, although the line may be difficult to draw.

While 'terrorism' or the unauthorized use of violence normally characterizes activities against an all-powerful state, which is why states are so readily persuaded to join forces to act against it, terrorist action can perhaps also be said to mark the reaction of states to such attempts at opposition. That is clear enough in the case of Nazi Germany during the Second World War, but it is also the case with some actions of colonial governments, in Algeria for example, where one can readily speak of state terrorism, both under colonial rule and afterwards. That is how many would see the recent actions of the Serbian government in Kosovo and elsewhere. Indeed, there may be some who would consider all repressive actions of the state, even those in accord with its own definitions of law and order, as forms of state terrorism. That is how they are seen by Western anarchists, and implicitly by fundamentalist Muslim Shiites, who in theory have no truck with civil authority (even in the form of rendering unto Caesar what is his). The same is effectively true of members of acephalous ('headless') societies ('tribes') in Africa and elsewhere when they set themselves against the power of the neighbouring states, just as the states were themselves in opposition to the chiefless peoples often seen as lawless bandits.

Terrorism is obviously differently valued depending on one's perspective. The Labour minister of defence in the Israeli cabinet described Ramallah as 'the capital of the terror' (*Le Monde*, 30 March 2002). Sharon's actions are aimed at destroying 'terrorism', and this is presumably one reason for the approval that the United States gives to these acts of revenge; Powell for example views the Palestinian attacks as being the cause of the events. The Arabs naturally take a different view, still defined in terms of terror. The prime minister of the Lebanon, Rafic Hariri, sees the actions of Sharon as designed to frustrate the peace initiatives proposed by the Saudis. 'The true terrorism', he declared, 'is what Israel is doing in the Palestinian territories.' The difference is clear and is even maintained in the most 'neutral' statements from the Western media. Palestinian fighters are nearly always referred to as terrorists, militants or gunmen, never as soldiers, the name applied to Israeli fighters (also gunmen like the others). It is the latter who have often been driven by extremist, religious views (Zionist, as distinct from the Puritanism, the extreme Protestantism, on which America was founded) at least as much as the Muslims.

The situation in Israel/Palestine is especially relevant to Europe, firstly, because Israel (and no other Near Eastern state) is defined as being within Europe for various cultural events, secondly, because the situation in Palestine is highly relevant to many Muslims in Europe and conditions their attitudes, leading to their willingness to take part in forms of violence. It cannot be doubted that events in Europe and the USA have been heavily influenced by what is happening in the Near East. In this respect the solidarity of Islam is different from that of other world religions.

The word 'gunman' is in general use for Palestinians and others who are deemed to be irregulars. It originates as a descriptive word, in opposition for example to 'pike-man' in the seventeenth century (a usage of 1624 according to the Oxford English Dictionary). The 1685 translation of Montaigne by Cotton writes of 'Gun-men of great ability and no common virtue' (II, 530). In the following century it became used above all of American Indians, who had of course acquired their guns from the Europeans. The Cherokees were said to have 3000 gunmen, not soldiers, a word reserved for the colonists or for the redcoats. So the term became applied above all to those who were not employed by the state or dressed in a uniform but who had the gun for other purposes, usually resisting oppression but sometimes for armed robbery.

It was in this sense that it became employed for Republicans in Ireland; though the IRA were occasionally called soldiers, they were more usually gunmen, as in Sean O'Casey's play *The Shadow of a Gunman*, whereas the Black and Tans were British (irregular) soldiers. In that play, the poet Davoren allows himself to be taken as a gunman by Millie and other residents of the same tenement, and in helping him Millie herself is killed, by one side or the other. Today it is the Israelis who have soldiers, whereas the Palestinians are referred to occasionally as militia but more usually as gunmen, a semantic usage perpetrated even by generally neutral commentators on the BBC World Service.

'Terrorist', then, turns out to be the label assigned to those who use illegal or illegitimate force against existing state authorities. They themselves are frequently people that see themselves as without justice, mostly without rights, whether political or property. That is why such an extraordinary variety of states have so avidly taken up the current American challenge to fight 'terrorism' – especially Israel, which condemns all Arab militancy as terrorist and likens it to the bombing of New York. Any national or minority movement that seeks to act against the state's monopoly of force can be so characterized, although such movements often do not see themselves as having any alternative mode of action. But there are also other groups with looser aims, not always political, the 'primitive bandits' of which Hobsbawm writes, the bandits of the Chinese 'water margins'. Even pirates could be considered terrorists in this sense, taking over the vessels of others by force and appropriating the contents as booty. Under some circumstances states encouraged this kind of activity against their enemies, as was the case with Francis Drake attacking Spanish ships in the Elizabethan period, for which he was honoured at home and desecrated abroad. Or the corsairs that preyed upon shipping in the Mediterranean.

Byron's travels in the eastern Mediterranean introduced him to piracy. In *The Bride of Abydos* he recounts how a law-defier becomes a law-abider. In *Don Juan* he returns to the same theme:

> Let not this mode of raising cash seem strong,
> Although he fleeced the flags of enemy nation,
> But into a prime minister but change
> His title, and 'tis nothing but taxation. (III, xiv)

Pirates and corsairs attacked the Ottoman forces in the Mediterranean, and the distinction between them and fighters for Greek independence was slight, if not invisible.

The difference with the other forms of 'terrorism' is that piracy was usually carried out for private pecuniary motives, much like those of the highwayman or indeed straightforward thieves on land. On the other hand, the example of Drake shows the state as encouraging such activity for its own purposes, which were partly political, even if only in the sense of strengthening its power and weakening that of its enemies. Many more recent cases of state 'terrorism' exist, such as those involving the encouragement by the CIA of armed opposition to governments in South America of which they did not approve, Allende in Chile or the Sandanistas in Nicaragua. Other examples, with a different political slant, come from Europe, where Western governments encouraged violence among opposition groups in Hungary and Czecho-slovakia under Russian over-rule. Here part of the justifica-tion was ideological, that they were aiding the struggle for freedom, just as in occupied Europe the Allies promoted attempts to harass the occupying forces.

There has been nothing to stop democratic powers them-selves from supporting so-called terrorist activity if they see it in their own short-term or long-term interest. In fact they have often aided such movements against other democratic governments, sometimes describing their action as promot-ing freedom. An obvious example of American support for terrorism was the help provided for Jewish organizations in the period leading up to (and following) 'independence', which saw the founding of the Jewish state of Israel on what had been Arab lands for the past 1500 years or more. The creation of the state of Israel transformed the status of the 'terrorists', at which point the illegal terrorist force became the army of the state. For the Palestinians the situ-ation was clearly different. In 1917 the British marched into this region, then under Turkish control, in support of the Arab rebellion but ended up establishing a Jewish homeland to be shared with the Palestinian inhabitants. The wander-ing Jew was relocated at the expense of the now homeless Arab, thus exporting, some were to say, Europe's problem to the Near East. The British were thus repeating what had happened in seventeenth-century North America, where colonial migrants from Europe established themselves on Indian land and drove many of the surviving Indians into reservations. Meanwhile the Palestinians have been demand-ing independence since the end of Turkish rule but were of course prevented from achieving that by the award of the mandated territory to the British by the League of Nations, by the Balfour Declaration promising the Jews a national homeland but specifically without prejudice to Palestinian rights, and by the strong support of America for increased immigration.

Many Palestinians were driven from their lands to end up in refugee camps in the Lebanon and in Jordan, which had taken over part of the previous mandated territory. As a result of the 1967 war, Israel conquered the whole of the West Bank of Jordan, former 'Palestinian' territory, and began to settle its own citizens in the occupied areas. Unlike the territory of Israel itself, there had been virtually no recent Jewish settlement in the area until then.

The Palestinians, left without a homeland, had to struggle against Israeli rule in order to regain the territory allocated to them (or to Jordan) as the result of the struggles after the Second World War, the outcome of which was recognized by the United States and by the international community. That was not the case with the occupation of the West Bank. Resolutions of the United Nations, which are still in force, call for Israel to evacuate that area and to return to its 1948 frontiers.

While the Palestinians have been given a measure of control over some of this territory, the region involved has been very limited, as have the powers granted to the authority. Some nations call for negotiation, but for Palestinians there can be no effective negotiations, only acceptance of the resolutions of the United Nations. Nor do they see Israel as willing to approximate to these. After all, the Israelis have had many years to comply and have had all the cards in their hands, that is, physical possession and a stupendous superiority of force. The main reason the Israelis want talks is to modify the international resolutions in their favour, negotiating from their position of strength. Given the failure of Israel to meet the demands of the United Nations, this unwillingness to agree to the wishes of the Palestinian peoples and the world, the failure of past negotiations, the pronouncement of Sharon and others, what are the subject peoples to do, many think, apart from to fall back on the use of illegitimate forms of force, on terrorism?

That situation might change when recognition is given to the state of Palestine, but such recognition seems unlikely to be forthcoming from the powers that wield overall power. How is the situation to be changed without simply waiting for something to happen and for 'terrorism' to continue? The recent conflict with Iraq has provided a slender fragment of hope that at least some Arab or Muslim nations might play a more positive role than they have done since the early days. Since Israel is supported by America, with its massive economic and military power, and Israel itself is well provided with weaponry (it has an army of twelve divisions, the second or third most powerful air force in the world, and nuclear weapons), any Palestinian state will need powerful allies, ready to come to its support. One possible but improbable scenario is for such powers to be called upon to establish the state of Palestine, to act beforehand in taking the initiative and policing the pre-1967 boundaries, to prevent Israelis coming into Palestinian lands by force and Palestinian combatants from attacking Israel, another version of an alliance against terrorism. The problem of colonies would be solved by giving Jews living in Palestine the same rights as Arabs living in Israel. That would mean taking the kind of pre-emptive action to resolve an international situation that the Anglo-Americans have justified in Iraq. It would on the other hand start off as a peaceful attempt to establish boundaries and the control of territory, but, given the protagonists, would have to be backed by the threat of force. Otherwise they would scarcely be effective as human shields.

In other words the defeat of terrorism involves the recourse to state-organized force, at least a peace force, and the mobilization of co-religionists in a Near Eastern campaign so that the Palestinians could reoccupy not the whole of their land but at least what remained in the 1948 settlement. That is to say, they would attempt to occupy as peacefully as possible the land taken from Jordan and the Palestinians at that time.

In such a struggle, the USA would support Israel, but such support might well have to take into account pressures from the oil-producing Arab states and possibly from the United Nations, which has already pronounced on this matter. But in this situation Europe should take the lead, since, unlike the rest of the Near East, Israel regards itself as a European power and participates on that basis in European competitions, in song contests, in football and academically. Like Turkey, but unlike its neighbours, it has associated membership of the European Union; but Turkey is at least partially in the continent of Europe. We have some responsibility in seeing that 'one of ours' obeys UN resolutions, as we had in the Balkans. In this case too we could help to turn a 'terrorist' movement into a legitimate struggle.

4

The Taliban, the Bamiyan and Us – the Islamic Other

Apart from the support given to the semi-secret military organization of al-Qaeda, the West has two abiding images of the Taliban – firstly, their closure of schools (and jobs) for women and, secondly, their destruction of the huge Buddhist statues in Bamiyan. I don't want to speak of the first except to say that they claim to have closed down schools pending a review of the curriculum for women. But there is of course a strong gender bias here, as in any educational system which is largely in the hands of male religious specialists who claim a special relationship with the scriptures, as was the case originally in Hinduism, in Christianity and in Judaism. With regard to the second, we were all (or almost all) appalled at the destruction of major works of art. It seems so barbaric, that total rejection of representation. And, from our contemporary standpoint, so it was. But is Islam really so very different?

The statues were destroyed by the legal government of the country who were applying an Islamic law (or what they saw as such). On 28 February 2001, an edict of Mullah Omar, leader of the movement, called for the destruction of idols throughout the Afghan territory. On 11 March the immense statues of Buddha, the largest in the world, constructed at Bamiyan on the ancient Silk Road running from

146

China to the West between 350 and 750 CE, were blown up by dynamite.

The very first statues of the Buddha were created during the Kuchan dynasty covering the period 45–350 CE, roughly that before Constantine and the conversion of the Roman Empire to Christianity. That dynasty saw the expansion from Peshawar in present-day Pakistan of the Graeco-Buddhist school, the art of which was obviously greatly influenced by the Greeks, who had been in the area since the conquests of Alexander the Great in 330–327 BCE. That followed some four hundred years after the Western thrust of the Persian emperor Cyrus II. The Greeks exported not simply a style, but the figurative image as such, at least to the Buddhists, who had hitherto never represented the Buddha in a figurative way. However, even in Greece where magnificent figurative sculpture dominated in the classical age, that great achievement followed the geometric period in which, as the name implies, figuration was avoided, possibly deliberately. And the classical age too gave birth to expressions of opposition, not only to figuration but to representation in general, in the works of Plato, notions that were later taken up by Protestants and by the precursors of the French Revolution (which was also initially iconoclastic) such as Rousseau in the eighteenth century. In other words there had been a degree of alternation between representation and its absence, ideologically and in practice.

To return to the Taliban, whatever they were politically, they were not mere barbarians, a word that we will find constantly coming up in this context, first from one side and then from the other. They had come on the scene in Afghanistan at a time when the various mujahedin factions, who had fought a religious war so successfully against the Soviet forces and who had been strongly supported by the USA, by the West and by Muslim nations everywhere, had begun seriously quarrelling amongst themselves, thus reducing an already devastated country to further chaos and ruin. In their effort to restore order, the Taliban received encouragement from the West. But in order to achieve their aim of neutralizing the various factions and of gathering in their arms, they adopted a radical programme, often described as fundamentalist, that is of going back to the fundamentals of Islam, which were in many ways very puritanical. In doing so, they took as models the Wahhabi movement of the Arabian peninsula, through which the present royal family, hardly the exemplar of puritanism, originally came to power, and which had also served as the model for the Senussi in North Africa. The latter had contributed to the ideological background for the fight against Italian occupation and to that of another hate figure of the West, who after a short-lived royalist regime succeeded the Italians in Libya, that is, Colonel Gaddafi, a man who also adopts a puritanical stance. Another model for the Taliban was the reformist movement in Iran directed against the shah and led by Ayatollah Khomeni, who again adopted a puritanical style when he returned to Iran. Such movements represented a wider body of people and groups which tended to oppose what they saw as the corruption and luxury of the West which was overwhelming them. A late nineteenth-century Gonja poet of West Africa called Al-Hajj Umar, who had spent some time in Arabia but composed in Hausa, wrote of what he described as the disaster that was coming to Africa from the West, from the Christians (the Nasallah, the Nazarenes). The poem became widely circulated and clearly represented a common way of thinking, though of course, as in Turkey and Egypt, there was much ambivalence about the coming of the West, of 'modernization'.

I have used the word 'puritanism' here in a general sociological sense, but the notion does have some relationship with the historical Puritans of New England and of Old Europe. The Protestant Reformation of the sixteenth century was itself puritanical in many respects. It propounded fundamentalist attitudes, which had been present in earlier protest movements such as the Lollards, the Hussites, and further back the Cathars and others, against the extravagances of the Catholic Church, in rich living (especially by the 'princes' of the Church), in loose living (of the celibate priesthood

148

and monks), in clothing (with elaborate ecclesiastical costumes), in art too (as in the case of the Medicis of Florence, of Cardinal Borromeo of Milan). They were returning, as they saw it, to the 'Word of God', to the Bible, to which all should have access (an important aspect of the history of education and of publishing) and to the simplicity of the early church, which included the rejection of riches (it is easier for a camel to pass through the eye of a needle than for a rich man to enter Heaven). These practices of the early church also included, for many, a rejection of representations, certainly in the theatre, which in its Roman and Greek forms ceased to exist, although in one sense it was replaced by ritual performances; they included as well some rejection of figurative representation, primarily of the three-dimensional kind (sculpture) but of painting too, mainly in ecclesiastical contexts but also in secular ones. Theatre and sculpture were two of the great artistic achievements of the Greeks, ones we now consider an intrinsic part of our Western heritage, yet they disappeared under, indeed were destroyed by, the Christian church, deliberately destroyed as a matter of ideology, as well as being rejected by Judaism and later by Islam.

Puritanism in the shape of iconoclasm has tended to mark the beginnings of world religions, which may in some cases allow figurative images later on. And in reformations and revolutions there is the same tendency to return to fundamentals, sometimes regarded as a form of extremism. This devotion to the word rather than the image in the early history of a world religion probably reflects the fact that these are founded upon written texts, and it is the word that distinguishes them from earlier image-based cults, now often regarded as concerned with idols.

This iconoclastic, puritanical approach to the world was revived by Protestants and especially by the Puritans, not only in New England but earlier in Old England too, under the dispensation of Edward VI in the middle of the sixteenth century and again later under the rule of Cromwell, the regicide and the leader of the English Revolution and of the

English Republic in the middle of the seventeenth. Under Cromwell, theatres were again closed and art was destroyed. Even Elizabeth, more tolerant in her Anglican compromise than others, had her ambassador tell the Sultan of Istanbul that both Islam and Protestantism were at one in rejecting icons. Now figurative art, even pictures with an entirely religious content, were banished. Some religious art from East Anglia, the home of the Mayflower emigrants, was sold to the more tolerant continent (Boldrick et al. 2002); beautiful medieval stained-glass windows were smashed to pieces in many of the parish churches in order to let in the pure light of God. Yes, here as elsewhere, there was a theological rationale for destruction. And it was a tradition that continued in many nonconformist churches in the West until very recently. The churches themselves were stripped, so too the churchyards. The latter had many of their existing monuments broken down and the new ones had at first no images at all, in New England for example, and even Christian images continued to be forbidden, although abstract and pagan ones were allowed. The cross, for example, was excluded – the Grecian urn or the skull and crossbones being used instead. That would have been to worship the dead rather than God. In the cemetery of Spanish Walls in the Bahamas, which I visited recently, inhabited by descendants of Puritan immigrants, there are no crosses, just plain headstones with simple inscriptions, as was the case in New England and indeed in most Protestant cemeteries before, in the Anglican Church, there was a return to the cross with the Anglo-Catholic ritual movement, the so-called Oxford Group, of the second half of the nineteenth century. In their asceticism, they resembled Jewish or Muslim burial places, bereft of figurative representations, of offerings, even of flowers. Similar objections were made in Islam. Ibn Taymuyah, a Hanbali living in Mamluk Damascus in the late thirteenth and early fourteenth century, called attention to the danger of legal changes that ignored the sharia. He objected for example to the reverence given to saints' tombs. The Mamluks imprisoned him and his movement died with him. But his ideas surfaced again in the revolutionary movement of the Wahhabis in the late eighteenth century which had such an influence in Arabia and in North Africa. Of course the movement against icons often has a specifically political aspect. In particular, new political movements may demand a new approach to iconography, a sweeping away of older forms. This happened during the English Revolution of 1649 and the French Revolution of 1789.

Now, in taking up such attitudes, the Protestants saw themselves as going back to early Christianity and to a set of iconoclastic and puritanical practices which had marked all three major Near Eastern religions, that is, Judaism, Christianity and Islam. The Islamic prohibition on representation, especially on figurative images, went back, as did the Christian, to the commandments of the Old Testament with their ban on graven images, secular as well as religious. It has sometimes been claimed that such attitudes are associated with the monotheistic creeds that characterized those Near Eastern religions. That is not, however, the case. For example, we find this same aversion to figurative images at an earlier stage of Buddhism, whose later statues the Taliban were so keen on destroying.

There were no figurative representations of the Buddha, of Sakyamuni, in early times. Buddhism first appeared in the fifth century BCE, and then the Buddha was represented only by his footprints, by a wheel or by the lotus, never in the figurative form in which we are so accustomed to seeing him in Buddhist art or in the more everyday context of Chinese shops, where the chubby figure is a symbol of wealth. What we now see as a highly iconic religion was at one time aniconic, opposed to the image. That transformation has occurred in other religions, though more rarely in Islam, which has had a stronger attachment to the old ways than other creeds. At that earlier time, Buddhist theologies had promulgated 'the doctrine of secret and holy non-duality of all existing things whatever their formal differences. They stressed the unity of exterior form and inner essence . . . the condition, degree . . . the form of a deity's spiritual presence in an image made by human hands were the subject of endless debate' (Brinker 2001: 20). The earliest canonical texts do not discuss the actual problem of the making of images, which is a frequent preoccupation of iconic religions, or of the manifestation of the Buddha in two or three 'bodies', as in later Mahayana doctrine.

The first of these bodies specified in that doctrine is 'the true body of the Dharma', the essence. In this body, the Buddha transcends all forms and cannot be represented in images or described in words; he is invisible and cannot be seen by the unenlightened. On the other hand, images for veneration could later be made of two other bodies, that of 'retribution', which was attained during the transmutation from bodhisattva, the future Buddha, to Buddha himself, and that of 'transformation', the shadow body in which the Buddha incarnates himself for the good of all unenlightened beings. Thus the Buddha fashions himself.

The oldest relevant text concerning this problem is the *Practice of the Way of Perfect Wisdom Scripture*, completed in 179, which states that the spirit of the Buddha is not present in his images. The image is made only so men can bow down and acquire merit. The Lianli dynasty (Buddhist) monk Sengyon (445–518) discussed the supposed journey of Laozi (the founder of Daoism) to India and wrote, in *Examining the Essay on Three-Fold Destruction*, 'The barbarians did not believe in emptiness (xu) and non-existence (wu). Therefore Laozi had statues made of the [Buddha's] form after he emigrated . . . and he converted [the barbarians with the help of these images].' That statement implies that at this time, for the Chinese too, images belonged to the barbarians, although they provided a way of converting the pagan who needed a visual supplement to the pure word. Literacy, the written word, the scriptures themselves, were not enough.

The ambivalence about image continued. An inscription on a Buddhist figure dated 746 proclaims 'The highest truth is without image. Yet if there was no image there would be no possibility for the truth to manifest itself. The highest principle is without words. Yet if there were no words how could the principle be known?' (Brinker 2001: 20).

The problem of the nature of the image's relationship to the deity is one that must raise itself in all iconic religions, since it concerns making the spiritual material or, more concretely, the invisible visible. The word of the scriptures is usually seen as in some way emanating directly from God, perhaps through the mouth of a prophet or of a messenger. The problem of the image arises because it is having to be repeatedly created in public, whereas the word has only to be copied, preferably by a cleric who can embellish nothing except by way of calligraphy. The image has more obviously to be created independently by human hands.

One solution is to give greater value, as in Hinduism, to images that are discovered or that appear in nature, just because they cannot be seen as having been created by human hands (acheiro-poidtes they were called in the Byzantine tradition; Brion 1996: 29). So too the word delivered on tablets of gold, as in the case of Joseph Smith and the Book of Mormon, or in stone as with Moses, solves the problem of the human creation of the text.

Yet another way is to recognize that the hand of man inevitably results in too great an element of materiality in representing the spiritual and hence to ban all representation as well as to destroy existing images. That is a very radical step to take but not altogether out of tune with views about the nature of the spiritual world, many of which border on the dualist, indeed on the Manichaean. For even in the very iconic religion of the Hindus, which in Vedic times was probably quite different in this respect, some Brahmans see the word of the scriptures, of which they are in charge both as reciters and as educators, as being much more important than the image, which is made primarily for the masses in situations of restricted literacy. That was also the case with the so-called Bible of the Poor in medieval Christianity, that is, the images that began to decorate the churches, especially after the resolution of the iconoclastic controversy at the Second Council of Nicaea in 787. And even among the generality of the users of images in Hinduism, there were problems about the relationship of the image to the deity. The images became the home of the god and able to receive offerings only when the eyes had been painted in during a special ceremony; and there was also controversy about whether the deity was permanently present or only there for the duration of the worship offered to it.

Doing away with the image of course resolves or avoids the whole problem of the material manifestation of the spiritual, and more specifically of humans creating gods rather than gods creating humans. For creating an image or a shrine for the deity raises, in acute form, the question of man or woman as the creator.

Yet at the same time as displaying this tendency to reject material images of the spiritual, making visible the invisible, hesitant mankind frequently calls for manifestations, often hard-copy representations, of the divine. That problem brings out the ambivalence, the contradiction, of the religious life, which becomes very explicit in the outsider's view, for example, in Protestant views of Catholicism. But even in Catholicism itself there was an internal critique, as of the more fleshly and erotic visions of some female mystics, who presented themselves as tasting Christ's foreskin and as enjoying his material as well as his spiritual love (Soskice 1996: 38). At the same time other pressures favoured a greater separation of the material and the spiritual, especially those that leant towards the Manichaean beliefs of the Cathars of Languedoc and of similar sects, where the material was identified with the world, the flesh and the devil.

The setting aside of iconophobia and the widespread emergence of images came in two modes. In Christianity, art became permitted if its theme was religious. It appeared in the cathedral of Marseilles as early as the fifth century CE. Outside the church, certainly in the great tradition (though not always in the folk tradition), virtually all painting and sculpture was religious in content until the Renaissance with its backward look to the secular, and indeed pagan, art of the classical period. It was the same with the rejection of the theatre. The initial return of drama seems to have been in the performances that grew out of the elaboration of worship, then in the mystery and miracle plays, and in England only much later, in the sixteenth century, to secular drama and the work of Marlowe, Shakespeare and the Elizabethan theatre.

In the Lebanon and elsewhere there was a similar but much less powerful movement towards dramatic representation in Islam and Judaism. Both religions banned the theatre, but Shiite Islam developed (apparently quite late) a miracle play centred on the murder of Ali, just as in Europe, under the influence of Christian developments, Judaism produced a type of miracle play centring upon the story of Esther and the Sukkoth harvest festival.

Otherwise, at least in the elite tradition, art under those religions developed in a secular, not in a religious, context. Islamic Persia, probably influenced by Chinese representations in the Central Asian cities such as Herat in Afghanistan, produced a secular art which was transmitted to India in the shape of Mughal painting, courtly, erotic, distinctly secular. That art developed at a time when the Muslim conquerors were destroying magnificent Hindu sculpture in temples and in step-wells.

I have spoken so far of the rejection of images in a religious context where the process is linked to notions of the opposition between the material and the spiritual, the visible and the invisible, as well as to ideas about the unique creation of the world by the High God. But the rejection did not stop there. It often applied to secular activity as well. In early Christianity, Judaism and Islam, it was not only religious images or theatre that were rejected but secular ones too. Indeed these categories were often hardly separable in those religions, since God had created all material life. In Islam for example the representation of natural objects was the representation of God's creation and hence a challenge to his supreme powers. Only the deliberate introduction of imperfections made them possible.

The Taliban, the Bamiyan and Us

I want very briefly to carry on the argument in three directions. Firstly by trying to show that these tendencies were present in other cultures, not only the written (although there, as always, the notions are more explicitly developed – that's the nature of the written word wherever found) but also, more surprisingly, the oral. Secondly I want to point to the parallel secular rejection of representation. And finally I want to ask very broadly why we find in so many human societies this kind of alternation between images and their absence, or even demolition.

Firstly to other cultures. There is nothing unique about the Near Eastern religions in respect of images. As we have seen, early Buddhism was aniconic like early Christianity. What about Hinduism? It is claimed the early Vedic religion was equally so. Certainly, as we have seen, there are some Brahmans today who are doubtful about the value of images; equally drama, except for the short period of the playwright Kalidas, was never an aspect of Hindu culture, apart from elaborate dance dramas such as Kathakali that take religious themes. They are basically people of the book, of the word, although they recognize that others need images.

China and Japan became the great centres of Buddhism, but that was always present in tandem with other creeds, especially Confucianism. In all of these cases there was some ambivalence about images as opposed to the word, in Zen Buddhism, for example, which was 'puritanical' in a number of ways, and in Confucianism, which firmly rejected ostentation. Mencius was much concerned over the gap between rich and poor, and that was one of many puritanical worries.

And while one might expect a greater elaboration of these doctrines in written cultures, one does, in my opinion, find the problem of ambivalence and contradiction present in oral ones as well. This is not the time or place to go into this question in detail, especially as I have written about it elsewhere (1997). But it seems to me highly significant that in African societies, where there is no question of the influence of the major world religions, you find throughout the continent a similar reluctance, as in Islam, Judaism and earlier Christianity (later Christianity is the one exception), about representing the High God. Even those African cultures that are highly iconic in their creation of wooden sculptures, as we know from all our ethnographic museums, do not offer figurative representations of the Creator, as if it were impossible to create the Creator, to render visible the ultimately invisible. Not only the High God but in some African cultures there is a reluctance to represent other important deities. And in a few, not I think influenced by Islam (although some were), to represent figuratively anything at all.

We have moved here from the first to the second question about secular art. In the classical world, Plato put forward a secular view of images when he declared himself against painting, for example, since what it offered was a lie. He had a special problem as he already thought that a material chair was a representation of the idea of a chair and could never be the ultimate reality. So that a painting was doubly misleading. The notion that representation, in general, is a lie, not simply in relation to the spiritual but to the secular, was taken up again by others, by Protestants of course but most prominently, in an intellectual way, by the eighteenth-century predecessors of the French Revolution. The founders of that revolution were heavily against representation, not merely painting and sculpture but also theatre. Much earlier French art was saved from destruction by being placed in the Louvre (ex-royal) museum, where it was accessible to the public, not simply to the rich. As for the theatre, the artificiality, the misrepresentation, of this art form, was rejected. When performances were eventually allowed, other than public celebrations, they had to take place against real rocks and trees, not ones painted on canvas or cardboard.

The third question I want to ask is, if such objections are not confined to the monotheistic religions, to written religions as a whole, and occur not only in oral cultures but later in secular ones, why should that be so? Combined with that question is the issue, raised by the critic Walter Benjamin, as to whether the modern age has seen the end of such ambivalence as a result of the dominance of images churned out by the printing press, the camera, film and TV. That thesis is I think partly true, but we do still get objections to image-making in the form of abstract art, in early twentieth-century Russia with Kandinsky and Malenkovitch, in Paris following the post-impressionists, in the USA with Pollock, Rothko and many others. The objections take the form of trying to discover a spiritual absolute, a purity in the absence of things.[1]

In my view this problem of images results from mankind's situation of being the symbolic animal, making a fundamental use of representations in their encounter with the world. Central to this use is language, which itself involves representation. But representations, whether in language or in images, are never the person, thing, or action itself. The word 'horse' is never the ridden horse, just as the word 'apple' or the picture 'apple' cannot be the eaten apple. Both word and image may in fact lead us into error.[2]

The topic I have discussed is a controversial one. It suggests that, in this apparently divisive respect, Islam in general, the Taliban in particular, shares a common heritage with us. In this context at least, it is a mistake to think of Islam as totally different from Judaeo-Christian civilization since it has many similar roots in the Old Testament. From other standpoints too it is incorrect to see Islam as the Other, since it has been based in Europe since the eighth century. And today there are possibly two million Muslims in Britain, two million in Germany and perhaps six million in France.

Pointing to similarities is not to deny we have values, preferences, of our own. I enjoy the cinema, the Taliban do not. Nevertheless, just as we may regard the destruction of the Buddhist statues as barbaric, so too they may regard their very existence as the work of barbarians! Indeed not only the Muslims but the Buddhists themselves took this view earlier on, and some in the Zen sect still do practise an intellectual puritanism of their own. And, as we have seen, it is very much part of our own traditions too. Coming on my maternal side from a Scottish Presbyterian background,

The Taliban, the Bamiyan and Us

the background of the New England meeting-house, I remember how, on early visits to France, I was appalled at the plethora of religious art, much of poor quality, that decorated Catholic churches (and indeed Orthodox ones as well, with their iconostases covered in icons). As an adolescent I was even more horrified at an Easter service in the Madeleine church in Paris on being asked to bend down and kiss the crown of thorns. Such representations, even without the worship, gave rise to feelings of revulsion just as profound as that of any Muslim.

We have changed. Increasing secularization, even globalization, has meant that the puritanical views of my mother's family are held by few. The city of Edinburgh, which once banned the theatre for two hundred or more years, now offers the world perhaps the most distinguished theatrical festival of them all; the Puritans of New England and the Jews of America, formerly rejecting not only theatrical representations but other artistic genres as well, are now world leaders in cinema, in theatre, in the whole array of artistic activity (even though the synagogue and the graveyard remain faithful to the rejection of images, as was true of the Puritans for many years). Times change and life becomes richer. America, which in the eighteenth century was a cultural desert (in the artistic sense), with a very thin culture of performance, has now become the major media culture of the world, exporting its products throughout the globe. The same was true to a lesser extent of France, where the revolution, picking up on a number of discussions of the eighteenth century, tried to get rid of the theatre and painting, both looked upon as largely aristocratic activities; then, as in the USA, the country became a major focus for the mass production of both.

We have to realize that, while representations of some kind, and language itself falls into that category, are essential for human life, not all forms have been essential at all times, and this is because representations always give rise to some kinds of doubt – doubts which in an extreme form were expressed in the destruction of the Bamiyan statues.

159

I have tried to cover a great deal of ground, perhaps too much, in a short space because I had in mind an attempt to outline the interaction between Europe and Islam, trying to point to what Islam had contributed, both positively and negatively, to that continent, as well as its similar roots to Judaism and Christianity. After having been largely repulsed, after many centuries Muslims have returned in mass to the continent, no longer as invaders but as immigrants. In both capacities they have had a lot to offer. Formerly they acted as a spur to the intellectual and scientific life, to the Renaissance itself. Now they provide an increasing part of the labour force that Europe needs to replenish its diminishing population. Both in the past and in the present Islam cannot be construed simply as the Other. Even in Asia, Muslim traditions are close to Christian and Jewish traditions. Muslims are very much part of the European scene.

Notes

1   For a seventeenth-century use of the notion of holy war in North Africa against the Muslims and in America against the Indians, see Matar 1999.
2   As a Hamas member recently remarked (*The Guardian*, 11 June 2002).

CHAPTER 1   PAST ENCOUNTERS

1   See García 1969.
2   Second Siege, in *The Poems of Mao Tse-Tung*, trans. W. Barnstone. London: Barrie & Jenkins, 1972.
3   For a semi-personal reconstruction of this trade, see A. Ghosh, *In an Antique Land* (London: Granta, 1992); otherwise of course the encyclopaedic works of S. D. Goitein.
4   For a more comprehensive account, see McCormick 2001. McCormick (2002) questions some aspects of the Pirenne thesis, but consensus reigns on the facts that 'the early eighth century marked the nadir of trade and shipping' in the Mediterranean, and the 'economic collapse of the Roman empire in the later sixth and seventh centuries. The trading networks linking Western Europe to the more developed economies of the Middle East were but shadows of their former selves, if

Notes

they still functioned at all' (p. 27). What became important was the slave trade to the Near East from the eighth century through which 'Europe financed the early growth of its commercial economy by selling Europeans as slaves to the Arab world' (p. 53).

5 See Martin 1900: vol. 1, p. 20. For a more general account, see Reinaud 1836.

6 In Italy silk-weaving spread to Lucca and then to Lyons and Northern Europe. It was earlier very important in southern Spain. Sugar spread not only to Italy and Spain but more significantly from there to Madeira, Brazil and the Caribbean.

7 The Khanate of Kipchak was later founded by Batu (*d. c.*1255), the grandson of Genghis Khan.

8 For a quasi-fictional account of the dispersal, see Amin Maalouf, *Leo the African*, trans. P. Sluglett. London: Quartet, *c.*1988.

9 German opinion can be gauged by the content of songs and pamphlets (*Flugschriften Zeitungen*) with titles such as *Dialogus de bello contra Turcos* (Leipzig 1529).

10 The Turks needed English tin for their armaments of bronze cannon.

11 The first English ambassador to Constantinople was commissioned in 1582 when the Armada was being prepared.

12 Quoted in J. Bronsted, *The Vikings* (Harmondsworth: Penguin, 1965, pp. 264–5).

13 You have to be clean to pray and you should pray five times a day. It is a common sight in West Africa to see Muslims going through the village with a kettle full of water, either for sanitary or for religious purposes.

14 De Martino 1988: 50. Constantine worked with one Joannis Saraceni.

15 Many Spanish names of scented plants come from the Arabic (as the English 'jasmine').

16 See Lemaires 2001.

17 Of the Center for History and Theory of Culture, Sofia, Bulgaria. Unpublished paper on the European impact and the transformation of the culinary culture in South-East Europe (the nineteenth century).

18 Kepel 1991: 113, on 'la naissance de l'Islam en France'.

19 See *Le Nouvel Observateur*, 8 Jan 2003, 'Musulmans en France: le défi islamiste'.

20 See the work of V. Ebin (*c.*1996) on the Murides.

Notes

CHAPTER 2   BITTER ICONS AND ETHNIC CLEANSING

1   The allusion is to Lawrence Durrell's account of an earlier and superficially less conflictual period of Cyprus history, entitled *Bitter Lemons*.
2   I am indebted to my host, Dr Paul Sant Cassia, for this and other observations.
3   I am indebted to the article by Hélène Despić-Popović in *Liberation*, 31 March 1999, p. 8.
4   See the report in the *New York Times*, 29 Oct 1999.

CHAPTER 3   ISLAM AND TERRORISM

1   J. A. Bush, Back to basics: the Law of War and the illegal fighter after September 11. *Ideas*, 9 (2002), 50–6.
2   See Matar 1999.

CHAPTER 4   THE TALIBAN, THE BAMIYAN AND US – THE ISLAMIC OTHER

1   See John Golding, *Paths to the Absolute* (London: Thames & Hudson, 2000) and the review by Jack Flam, 'Space Men', in the *New York Review of Books*, 48 (2001), 10–14.
2   In a recent article entitled 'The Voice of Marble', the art critic Leonard Barkan wrote: 'the very basis of recuperating ancient sculpture that represented human form [what I call figurative representation] was to endow the object with a voice' (Barkan 1999: xxiv); he speaks of 'the fiction of an apostrophe to an absent . . . entity' and conferring the powers of speech. We know what he means; he is talking metaphorically about what it can tell us, but it is nevertheless representing reality too really and hence a fiction, perhaps a lie (Serra 2002: 65).

References and Bibliography

Abulafia, D. 1994. *A Mediterranean Emporium: The Catalan Kingdom of Majorca*. Cambridge: Cambridge University Press.

Allievi, S. 1994. Le retour de l'Islam: la présence musulmane entre histoire et actualité. *Bulletin de l'Institut de Recherche sur le Maghreb Contemporain* (IRMC), NS 22/3, 3–8.

Allievi, S., and Dassetto, F. 1993. *Il ritorno dell' Islam: i Musulmani in Italia*. Rome: Lavoro.

Ancién, M. et al. 1998. *L'Islam i Catalunya*. Barcelona: Lunwerg.

Armani, M. 1935. *Storia del Musulmani di Sicilia*, 2nd edn, 3 vols. Catania.

Barkan, L. 1999. *Unearthing the Past: Archaeology and Aesthetics in the Making of Renaissance Culture*. New Haven: Yale University Press.

Bell, J. N. 1979. *Love Theory in Later Hanbalite Islam*. Albany: State University of New York Press.

Birmingham, D. 1993. *A Concise History of Portugal*. Cambridge: Cambridge University Press.

Boase, R. 1977. *The Origin and Meaning of Courtly Love*. Manchester: Manchester University Press.

Boase, R. 1989. The disputed heritage: Europe's cultural debt to the Arabs. *Bulletin of Hispanic Studies*, 66.

Boase, R. 1994. Arab influences on European love-poetry. In S. K. Jayyusi (ed.) *The Legacy of Muslim Spain*. Leiden: Brill.

Boldrick, S., Park, D., and Williamson, P. (eds) 2002. *Wonder: Painted Sculpture from Medieval England*. Leeds: Henry Moore Institute.

References and Bibliography

Braudel, F. 1972–3. *The Mediterranean and the Mediterranean World in the Age of Philip II*, trans. S. Reynolds. London: Collins.

Briggs, M. S. 1931. Architecture. In T. Arnold and A. Guillaume (eds) *The Legacy of Islam*. Oxford: Clarendon Press, 155–79.

Briggs, M. S. 1933. Gothic architecture and Persian origins. *Burlington Magazine*, 1, 183–9.

Brinker, H. 2001. Early Buddhist art in China. In L. Michel (ed.) *The Return of the Buddha: The Qingshou Discoveries*. London: Royal Academy of Arts.

Brion, M. 1996. *Les Peintres de Dieu*. Paris.

Brough, J. 1968. *Poems from the Sanskrit*. Harmondsworth: Penguin.

Bürgel, J. C. 1988. *The Feather of Simurgh: The 'Licit Magic' of the Arts in Medieval Islam*. New York: New York University Press.

Bürgel, J. C. 1994. Ecstasy and control in Andalusi art: steps towards a new approach. In S. K. Jayyusi (ed.) *The Legacy of Muslim Spain*. Leiden: Brill.

Burke, P. 1998. *The European Renaissance: Centres and Peripheries*. Oxford: Blackwell.

Burnett, C. 1997. *The Introduction of Arabic Learning into England*. London: British Library.

Burton, R. F. 1894. *The Book of the Thousand Nights and a Night*, 12 vols. London: Nichols.

Campbell, D. 1926. *Arabian Medicine and its Influence on the Middle Ages*. London: Kegan Paul.

Cardini, F. 1999. *Europe and Islam*. Oxford: Blackwell.

Christensen, E. 1980. *The Northern Crusades: The Baltic and the Catholic Frontier, 1100–1525*. New York: Macmillan.

Colley, L. 2002. *Captives, Britain, Empire and the World 1600–1850*. London: Cape.

Constable, O. R. 1994. Muslim merchants in Andalusi international trade. In S. K. Jayyusi (ed.) *The Legacy of Muslim Spain*. Leiden: Brill.

Daniel, N. 1962. *Islam and the West: The Making of an Image*. Edinburgh: Edinburgh University Press.

Daniel, N. 1975. *The Arabs and Mediaeval Europe*. London: Longman.

de Castro, T. 2002. L'émergence d'une identité alimentaire: musulmans et chrétiens dans la royaume de Grenade. In M. Bruegel and B. Laurioux (eds) *Histoire et identités alimentaires en Europe*. Paris: Hachette.

References and Bibliography

de Martino, A. 1988. Constantino Africano. In M. Pasca (ed.) *La scuola medica Salernitana: storia, immagini, manoscritti del' XI al XIII secolo*. Naples: Electa.

Despić-Popović, H. 1999. article in *Liberation*, 31 March.

Dickie, J. 1994. Granada: a case study of Arab urbanism in Muslim Spain. In S. K. Jayyusi (ed.) *The Legacy of Muslim Spain*. Leiden: Brill.

Dodds, J. 1994a. The mudejar tradition of architecture. In S. K. Jayyusi (ed.) *The Legacy of Muslim Spain*. Leiden: Brill.

Dodds, J. 1994b. The arts of al-Andalus. In S. K. Jayyusi (ed.) *The Legacy of Muslim Spain*. Leiden: Brill.

Dozy, R. 1913. *Spanish Islam: A History of the Moslems in Spain*, trans. F. G. Stokes. London: Chatto & Windus.

Dumont, H. 1970. *Homo hierarchicus: The Caste System and its Implications*, trans. M. Sainsbury. London: Weidenfeld & Nicolson.

Durrell, L. 1959. *Bitter Lemons*. London: Faber.

Eagleton, T. 1999. Nationalism and the case of Ireland. *New Left Review*, 234, 4–61.

Ebin, V. 1996. Making room versus creating space. In B. Metcalf (ed.) *Making Muslim Space in North America and Europe*. Berkeley: University of California Press.

Edwards, D. 2003. Caravans of martyrs: sacrifice in Afghanistan. Paper given at the conference on 'Cultures of Violence?', St John's College, Cambridge.

Finley, M. I., Mack Smith, D., and Duggan, C. 1986. *A History of Sicily*. London: Chatto & Windus.

Fischer-Galati, S. A. 1959. *Ottoman Imperialism and German Protestantism*. Cambridge, MA: Harvard University Press.

Fisher, G. 1957. *Barbary Legend*. Oxford: Clarendon Press.

Frazer, J. 1890. *The Golden Bough: A Study in Magic and Religion*, 2 vols. London: Macmillan.

Gabrieli, F. (ed.) 1983. *Histoire et civilisation de l'Islam en Europe: Arabes et Turcs en Occident du VIIe au XXe siècle*. Paris: Bordas.

García, E. 2002. La diététique arabe, reflet d'une réalité quotidienne ou d'une tradition fossilisée. Paper given at the conference of the IEHA, Tours, December 2002.

García, P. G. 1992. Análisis de las Antiguas 'Relaciones de Moros y Christianos de Laroles' (La Alpujarra). *Gazeta de Antropología*, 9.

Geanakoplos, D. J. 1962. *Greek Scholars in Venice*. Cambridge, MA: Harvard University Press.

References and Bibliography

Geanakoplos, D. J. 1966. *Byzantine East and Latin West*. Oxford: Blackwell.

Gellner, E. 1963. Sanctity, Puritanism, secularization and nationalism in North Africa. *Archives de Sociologie des Religions*, 8, 71–86.

Gellner, E. 1968. A pendulum swing theory of Islam. *Annales Marocaines de Sociologie*, 4–14.

Gellner, E. 1983. *Nations and Nationalism*. Oxford: Blackwell.

Gernet, J. [1972] 1982. *A History of Chinese Civilization*. Cambridge: Cambridge University Press.

Gibbon, E. [1776–88] 1887. *The History of the Decline and Fall of the Roman Empire*. London.

Giddens, A. 1985. *A Contemporary Critique of Historical Materialism*, vol. 2: *The Nation-State and Violence*. Cambridge: Polity.

Giffen, L. A. 1971. *Theory of Profane Love among the Arabs: The Development of the Genre*. New York: New York University Press.

Glick, T. F. 1970. *Irrigation and Society in Medieval Valencia*. Cambridge, MA: Harvard University Press.

Glick, T. F. 1979. *Islamic and Christian Spain in the Early Middle Ages: Comparative Perspectives on Social and Cultural Formations*. Princeton: Princeton University Press.

Goody, J. 1983. *The Development of the Family and Marriage in Europe*. Cambridge: Cambridge University Press.

Goody, J. 1997. *Representations and Contradictions: Ambivalence towards Images, Theatre, Fiction, Relics and Sexuality*. Oxford: Blackwell.

Goody, J. 1998. *Food and Love*. London: Verso.

Grabar, O. 1994. Two paradoxes in the Islamic art of the Spanish peninsula. In S. K. Jayyusi (ed.) *The Legacy of Muslim Spain*. Leiden: Brill.

Guichard, P. 1977. *Structures sociales 'orientales' et 'occidentales' dans l'Espagne musulmane*. Paris: Mouton.

Guichard, P. 1994. The social history of Muslim Spain. In S. K. Jayyusi (ed.) *The Legacy of Muslim Spain*. Leiden: Brill.

Gustavino Gallent, G. 1969. *La fiesta de Moros y Christianos y su problemática*. Madrid.

Halliday, F. 1995. *Islam and the Myth of Confrontation: Religion and Politics in the Middle East*. London: Tauris.

Hamilton, A. 2001. *Arab Culture and Ottoman Magnificence in Antwerp's Golden Age*. Oxford: Oxford University Press.

Haskins, C. H. 1924. *Studies in the History of Mediaeval Science*. Cambridge, MA: Harvard University Press.

References and Bibliography

Haskins, C. H. 1927. *The Renaissance of the Twelfth Century.* New York.

Hasluck, M. 1954. *The Unwritten Law in Albania.* Cambridge: Cambridge University Press.

Heyberger, B. 2002. Les Européens vus par les Libanais (XVIe–XIXe siècles). In B. Heyberger and C.-M. Welbiner, *Les Européens vus par les Libanais à l'époque ottoman.* Beirut.

Hibbert, C. [1974] 1979. *The Rise and Fall of the House of Medici.* Harmondsworth: Penguin.

Hillenbrand, R. 1994. 'The ornament of the world': medieval Cordoba as a cultural centre. In S. K. Jayyusi (ed.) *The Legacy of Muslim Spain.* Leiden: Brill.

Hobsbawm, E. 1990. *Nations and Nationalism since 1780.* Cambridge: Cambridge University Press.

Hodges, R., and Whitehouse, D. 1983. *Mohammed, Charlemagne and the Origins of Europe.* London: Duckworth.

Howard, D. 2000. *Venice and the East: The Impact of the Islamic World on Venetian Architecture 1100–1500.* New Haven: Yale University Press.

Ibn Hazm 1953. *The Ring of the Dove: A Treatise on the Art and Practice of Arab Love,* trans. A. J. Arberry. London: Luzac.

Jacquart, D., and Micheau, F. 1990. *La Médecine arabe et l'Occident médiéval.* Paris: Maisonneuve & Larose.

Jardine, L., and Brotton, J. 2000. *Global Interests: Renaissance Art between East and West.* London: Reaktion.

Jayyusi, S. K. (ed.) 1994. *The Legacy of Muslim Spain.* Leiden: Brill.

Kaltanbach, J.-H., and Tribalat, M. 2002. *La République et l'Islam: entre crainte et aveuglement.* Paris: Gallimard.

Kepel, G. [1987] 1991. *Les Banlieues de l'Islam: naissance d'une religion en France.* Paris: Le Seuil.

Khosrokhavar, F. 1995. *Le Foulard et la République.* Paris: La Découverte.

Khosrokhavar, F. 1997. *L'Islam des jeunes.* Paris: Flammarion.

Khosrokhavar, F. 2002. *Les Nouveaux Martyrs d'Allah.* Paris: Flammarion.

Lemaires, G.-G. 2001. *The Orient in Western Art.* Cologne.

Leveau, R., and Mohsen-Finan, K. 2001. France-Allemagne: nouvelles perspectives, identités et sociétés. In R. Leveau, K. Mohsen-Finan and C. Wihtol de Wenden, *L'Islam en France et en Allemagne: identités et citoyennetés.* Paris: La Documentation française.

168

References and Bibliography

Lévi-Provençal, E. 1931. *L'Espagne musulmane en Xe siècle*. Paris: Maisonneuve & Larose.

Lewis, A. 1958. The closing of the European frontier. *Spectrum*, 33.

Lewis, B. 1982. *The Muslim Discovery of Europe*. New York and London: W. W. Norton.

Lewis, B. 1993. *Islam and the West*. Oxford: Oxford University Press.

Lewis, B., and Schnapper, D. (eds) 1992. *Musulmans en Europe*. Arles: Actes Sud.

Linehan, P. 2001. At the Spanish frontier. In P. Linehan and J. L. Nelson (eds), *The Medieval World*. London: Routledge.

López-Baralt, L. 1994. The legacy of Islam in Spanish literature. In S. K. Jayyusi (ed.) *The Legacy of Muslim Spain*. Leiden: Brill.

Lynch, J. 1965. *Spain under the Habsburgs*. Oxford: Blackwell.

McCormick, M. 2001. *Origins of the European Economy: Communications and Commerce AD 300–900*. Cambridge: Cambridge University Press.

McCormick, M. 2002. New light on the 'Dark Ages': how the slave trade fuelled the Carolingian economy. *Past and Present*, 177, 17–54.

McEvedy, C. 1992. *New Penguin Atlas of Medieval History*. Harmondsworth: Penguin.

Mahdi, M. 1984. *The Thousand and One Nights from the Earliest Sources*. Leiden: Brill.

Malcolm, N. 1998. *Kosovo: A Short History*. London: Macmillan.

Markovits, C. 2000. *The Global World of Indian Merchants 1750–1947: Traders of Sind from Bukhara to Panama*. Cambridge: Cambridge University Press.

Martin, E. 1900. *Histoire de la ville de Lodève*. Montpellier: Lecoeur.

Matar, N. 1999. *Turks, Moors and Englishmen in the Age of Discovery*. New York: Columbia University Press.

Menocal, M. R. 1987. *The Arabic Role in Medieval Literary History: A Forgotten Heritage*. Philadelphia: University of Pennsylvania Press.

Metlitzki, D. 1977. *The Matter of Araby in Medieval England*. New Haven: Yale University Press.

Montaigne, M. 1685. *Essays*, trans. C. Cotton. London: Gillyflower.

Nakosteen, M. K., and Szyliowicz, J. S. 1997. History of education (Muslim). *In Encylopaedia Britannica*, 15th edn, vol. 18, 16–17.

Nykl, A. R. 1946. *Hispano-Arab Poetry and its Relations with the Old Provençal Troubadours*. Baltimore: J. H. Furst.

169

References and Bibliography

O'Brien, D. B. C. 1971. *The Mourides of Senegal: The Political and Economic Organization of an Islamic Brotherhood*. Oxford: Clarendon Press.

Pacey, A. 1990. *Technology in World Civilization*. Cambridge, MA: MIT Press.

Parrain, C. 1964. Rapports de production et développement des forces productives: l'example du moulin à eau. *La Pensée*, 115, 55–70.

Pirenne, H. 1939. *Mohammed and Charlemagne*, trans. B. Miall. London: Allen & Unwin.

Prutz, H. 1883. *Die Kulturgeschichte der Kreuzzuge*. Berlin.

Pryor, J. H. 1988. *Geography, Technology and War: Studies in the Maritime History of the Mediterranean 649–1571*. Cambridge: Cambridge University Press.

Rath, J. et al. 2001. *Western Europe and its Islam*. Leiden.

Reinaud, J. T. 1836. *Invasions des Sarrazins en France et de France en Savoie, en Piémont et dans la Suisse, pendant les VIIIe, IXe et Xe siècles de notre ère, d'après des auteurs chrétiens et mahometans*. Paris.

Robb, P. 1996. *Midnight in Sicily*. London: Harvill Press.

Roden, C. 1985. *A New Book of Middle Eastern Food*. Harmondsworth: Penguin.

Rodinson, M. 1980. *La Fascination de l'Islam*. Paris.

Runciman, S. 1969. *A History of the Crusades*, ed. K. M. Selton, 2nd edn. Madison.

Said, E. 1978. *Orientalism*. New York: Pantheon.

Sant Cassia, P. (forthcoming). *Memories of Conflict*. Oxford.

Saynes, J. et al. 1986. *Histoire de Béziers*. Toulouse.

Sells, M. A. 1996. *The Bridge Betrayed: Religion and Genocide in Bosnia*. Berkeley: University of California Press.

Sen, F. 2002. *Islam in Deutschland*. Munich: Beck.

Serra, I. 2002. The voice of marble: prosopopoeic of the past in present Italy. *Florida Atlantic Comparative Studies*, 5, 65–80.

Soskice, J. M. 1996. Sight and vision in medieval Christian thought. In T. Brennan and M. Jay (eds) *Vision in Context*. New York and London: Routledge.

Southern, R. 1978. *Western Views of Islam in the Middle Ages*. Cambridge, MA: Harvard University Press.

Stimson, D. (ed.) 1962. *Sarton on the History of Science*. Cambridge, MA: Harvard University Press.

References and Bibliography

Tasso, T. [1600] 1853. *Jerusalem Recovered*, trans. E. Fairfax. London.

Terrasse, M. 2001. *Islam et Occident méditerranéen: de la conquête aux Ottomans*. Paris: Comité des travaux historiques et scientifiques.

Tietze, N. 2001. 'Être musulman' en France et en Allemagne. In R. Leveau, K. Mohsen-Finan and C. Wihtol de Wenden, *L'Islam en France et en Allemagne: identités et citoyennetés*. Paris: La Documentation française.

Toaff, A. 2000. *Mangiare alla Giudia*. Bologna.

Torres, C., and Macias, S. 1998. *O legado Islâmico em Portugal*. Lisbon: Fundação Circulo Leitores.

Vernet, J. 1985. *Ce que la culture doit aux Arabes d'Espagne*. Paris.

Vernet, J. 1994. Natural and technical sciences in al-Andalus. In S. K. Jayyusi (ed.) *The Legacy of Muslim Spain*. Leiden: Brill.

Viguera, M. 1994. Aṣluḥu li 'l-maʿālī: on the social status of Andalusī women. In S. K. Jayyusi (ed.) *The Legacy of Muslim Spain*. Leiden: Brill.

Wachtel, N. 1971. *Los vencidos: los indios del Perú frente a la conquista española (1530–1570)*. Madrid.

Waines, D. 1989. *In a Caliph's Kitchen: The Golden Age of the Arab Table*. London: Riad El-Rayyes.

Wallerstein, I. 1974. *The Modern World-System*. New York and London: Academic Press.

Warton, T. [1774] 1871. *History of English Poetry from the Twelfth to the Close of the Sixteenth Century*, ed. R. C. Hezlitt. London: Reeves & Tanner.

Watt, W. M. 1991. *Muslim–Christian Encounters*. London: Routledge.

Wickham, C. 1994. *Land and Power: Studies in Italian and European Social History, 400–1200*. London: British School at Rome.

Wright, O. 1994. Music in Islamic Spain. In S. K. Jayyusi (ed.) *The Legacy of Muslim Spain*. Leiden: Brill.

Yahya, D. 1981. *Morocco in the Sixteenth Century*. Harlow: Longman.

Yalman, N. 2001. Further observations on love. *Cultural Horizons: A Festschrift in Honor of Talat S. Halman*, ed. J. L. Warner. Syracuse, NY: Syracuse University Press.

Zafrani, H. 1996. *Juifs d'Andalousie et du Maghreb*. Paris: Maisonneuve & Larose.

Index

Index

Index